THEN AND THERE SERIES
GENERAL EDITOR
MARJORIE REEVES M.A. PH.D.

Scotland in the Days of Burns

HYMAN SHAPIRO

Illustrated from contemporary sources

LONGMAN

LONGMAN GROUP LTD
LONDON

*Associated companies, branches and representatives
throughout the world*

© Longman Group Ltd 1968
First published 1968
Fourth impression 1973

ISBN 0 582 20419 4
Printed in Hong Kong by Wing Tai Cheung Printing Co Ltd

FOR DAVID, JESSICA AND JUDITH

ACKNOWLEDGEMENTS

The author wishes to thank Mr Robert Wilkie, the Curator of the Old
Glasgow Museum; the Tam O' Shanter Museum, Ayr; the Attendants
of the Mitchell Library, Glasgow, and of the Old Edinburgh Room in
Edinburgh Public Library, and the Scottish National Portrait Gallery,
Edinburgh.

For permission to reproduce photographs we are grateful to the
following:—Aerofilms Ltd.—page 78 top; Burns' Cottage, Alloway,
and Collins' edition of the Poems of Burns—page 92; J. Allan Cash—
pages 36 and 75; Dalling and Henderson Ltd.—page 56; Faculty of
Advocates—page 98; Glasgow Art Gallery and Museum—pages 3, 81,
82 and 89; The Trustees of the Goodwood Collection—page 32;
Mansell Collection—pages 11 bottom, 20, 65, 87 and 104; Earl of
Mansfield—page 58 top; Ministry of Public Building and Works
(Crown Copyright)—page 72; National Coal Board—page 91;
National Gallery of Scotland—pages 7, 33, 39, 49, 54, 55, 57, 58
bottom and 100; The Trustees of the National Library of Scotland—
page 10; National Maritime Museum, Greenwich—page 86; National
Monuments Record of Scotland—page 76; National Museum of
Antiquities, Scotland—page 31; George Outram & Co. Ltd—page 26;
Radio Times Hulton Picture Library—pages 4, 11 top, 25, 50, and 94;
The University of Reading, Museum of English Rural Life—pages 5
top and 17; Science Museum, London (Crown Copyright)—page 88
top; Tom Scott—page 74; Scottish National Portrait Gallery—page 1;
Countess of Swinton (photograph supplied by Manchester City Art
Galleries)—page 5 bottom.
The illustrations on pages v, 8, 13, 19, 34, 47, 62-63, 67, 88 bottom,
93 and 101 are from copies in The Mitchell Library, Glasgow; that
on page 43 from T. C. Lethbridge, *Boats and Boatmen* (Thames and
Hudson), and the map on page 30 has been redrawn from W. R.
Kermack, *The Scottish Highlands* (W. and A. K. Johnston and G. W.
Bacon Ltd.)

CONTENTS

TO THE READER

As you read this book try to imagine the Scotland of two hundred years ago. There were no fields of hay, clover, potatoes and turnips. The corn and barley was poor-looking stuff. We should not recognise in the shambling skinny cows the ancestors of our Ayrshires and Galloways, nor in the stunted sheep those of our Cheviots and Blackfaced. Where we now see prosperous farm steadings with tractors and combine-harvesters, there were tumble down hovels and clumsy ploughs. There were few trees and hedges, and no fences. Rough pasturage, moorland and marsh stretched in all directions beyond the strips of tilled ground. No railways cut across the countryside, and instead of the hard-surfaced roads that we whiz over today, we should be lucky if we could find bridle paths or rutted lanes where even to lead a farm cart would be a risky undertaking.

The contrast between the towns of then and now is even more startling. I have not, however, dealt with that in this book, for it is covered in two other 'Then and There' books: 'Glasgow and the Tobacco Lords' and 'Edinburgh in its Golden Age'.

How do we know what Scotland was like in those far off days? There are, of course, mountains of government reports, council and church records, and parish registers. Quite a number of people wrote of their own days and histories of what was happening in their time. Visitors from overseas and England wrote of what they saw, and ambassadors sent accounts to their own governments. We have collections of

THE

STATISTICAL ACCOUNT

OF

SCOTLAND.

DRAWN UP FROM THE COMMUNICATIONS

OF THE

MINISTERS

OF THE

DIFFERENT PARISHES.

By Sir JOHN SINCLAIR, Bart.

VOLUME FIFTH.

" *Ad consilium de republica dandum, caput est nosse rempublicam.*"
CICERO de Orat. lib. ii.

EDINBURGH:

PRINTED AND SOLD BY WILLIAM CREECH;
AND ALSO SOLD BY J. DONALDSON, A. GUTHRIE, W. LAING, AND
JO. AND JA. FAIRBAIRN, EDINBURGH ; T. CADELL,
J. DEBRETT, AND J. SEWEL, LONDON;
DUNLOP AND WILSON, GLASGOW; AND
ANGUS AND SON, ABERDEEN.

M,DCC,XCIII.

V

letters, family papers, and files of newspapers, especially from the second half of the century, that tell us a great deal.

The most complete record of conditions in eighteenth-century Scotland is 'The Statistical Survey of Scotland', published in twenty-two volumes between 1791 and 1800. Sir John Sinclair, its editor, had sent a long letter to every parish minister in the country asking for answers to a great number of questions—about the geography of the parish, its history, population, industries, farming methods, customs, health conditions, schools, and so on. He received very full replies, and printed them as they arrived. They are a mine of information. I am quite sure that the main library in your town or county will have a set. You will find it exciting and entertaining to read the accounts of the places that interest you.

Many glimpses of the period are to be found in stories and poems. John Galt's 'Annals of the Parish' is a revealing and amusing story of the life of a minister in an Ayrshire town. Sir Walter Scott's novels 'Rob Roy' and 'Waverley' show us what the Highlands were like. In the poems of Burns, and in his letters and journals we have a wealth of information about the people around him, their homes, customs, poverty, loves and hates, revolt against injustice, and hopes for the future.

On the shelves of the public library there will be a number of books written by historians who have made a special study of that time. Two that you might look for are P. Hume Brown's 'Early Travellers in Scotland' and H. Grey Graham's 'Social Life of Scotland in the Eighteenth Century'.

Words printed *in italics* are explained in the Glossary, page 105.

1 The Background of a Farmer Poet

Portrait of Robert Burns by his friend Alexander Nasmyth

On a bleak day in 1740 nineteen-year-old William Burns stood with his brother Robert on a hilltop in Kincardine. This was the parting of their ways. Robert was setting off for Montrose to seek a job as a mason. William, a gardener, was going to try his luck in Edinburgh.

Many a country lad was leaving home in those days. Some made for the Lowland towns where, they had heard, though you might be poor you did not starve. Some, with a sack of

1

oatmeal to keep them going on their long voyage, trudged to Campbeltown or Greenock, and crowded on a tiny ship to get land and freedom in America. Others, with no money for the fare, sold themselves into seven years' slavery on a sugar 'or tobacco plantation in the West Indies or Virginia. The most adventurous and enterprising Scotsmen were leaving their homes, for there was no living to be had in their native land.

The father of these two young men was a gardener who, as his laird's man, had fought for the Stewarts in the 1715 Rebellion. When his master was exiled he rented a farm of his own, but lost it when he could not repay the money he had borrowed. Ambitious for his children, he had encouraged his neighbours to join with him in building a hut for a school and engaging a teacher. When he lost his farm his sons had to fend for themselves.

Seventeen-forty was a year of famine. William and Robert had seen people grovelling for weeds to stave off the gnawing pangs of hunger. They had listened to their elders' tales of the seven wet sunless years round about 1700 when thousands had died of starvation, and the survivors had been too weak to bury them. So the two lads shouldered their packs and strode off to look for a living. Here we must leave Robert, and follow the fortunes of William.

After two years in Edinburgh William made his way to Ayrshire. He rented seven acres in Alloway for a vegetable garden, built a house on his land, and married a local girl. Here his son Robert, who was to become Scotland's greatest poet, was born on the twenty-fifth of January 1759.

The house is still there, furnished much as it was then. It has a living room, kitchen and byre. Some improvements have been made. The roof is now thatched with straw instead of turf, and the chimney heads have been renewed. The windows have been enlarged, with glass in the lower parts instead of

The cottage in Alloway where Burns was born

wooden shutters. Thousands of people from all over the world visit it every year. If you would like to catch a glimpse of eighteenth-century Scotland, you too should pay it a visit.

The Burns family lived here for seven years. William was kept busy working on the estates of neighbouring landowners. One of these was the Provost of Ayr, Dr. Ferguson. He had made a fortune in London treating wealthy patients, and had retired to his native county. He bought a large estate, built a fine mansion on it, and hired William to lay out the garden, and plant woods and shrubberies. William did the job so well and conscientiously that Dr Ferguson offered him the lease of a seventy-acre holding, Mount Oliphant, nearby, but at a rent six times what it had been worth when he had bought it. William now had a family of four—Robert, aged seven, Gilbert a year younger, and two little girls. Like his own father, he wanted to improve the children's chances in life, and the prospect of having a farm was a great temptation. The money he had saved, however, was not nearly enough to

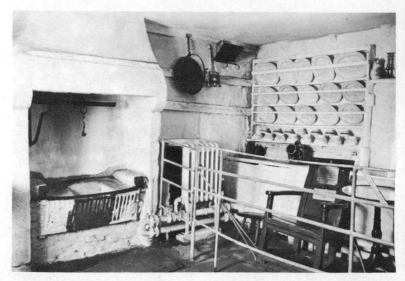

The kitchen of Burns's Cottage—The radiator to the right of the fireplace is a modern addition

buy the fertilisers and lime and seed and cattle and sheep and implements and everything else that would be needed. Dr Ferguson offered him a loan of £100 to help him to make a start, and William, after giving the matter much thought, agreed to become the tenant of Mount Oliphant.

Before long he was regretting the decision. The hollows were marshy, and the soil was lifeless and sour. Year after year the crops were scanty, and it became obvious that it would take a lot of time and money, and much hard labour, before the ground could be improved. He could not afford to hire a farmhand, and the two little boys had to do a man's work. They goaded the horses, cleared the stones from the path of the ploughshare, helped with the sowing, weeding, reaping and threshing. This last was the hardest task of all. The flail was made of two heavy pieces of wood hinged together with leather, and had to be brought down with great force on the corn, pounding it until the seed was separated from the husk.

4

In the cottage at Alloway, there is a flail like the one Burns used.

When Dr Ferguson died his factor demanded immediate payment of the arrears of rent and the £100 loan. The family was in despair. Later, in a poem, 'The Twa Dogs', Burns bitterly recalled how 'Poor tenant bodies, scant o' cash', had 'to thole the factor's snash' (suffer his insolence) while he would 'stamp and threaten, curse and swear' to arrest them and confiscate their goods.

A flail

Suffering 'the cheerless gloom of a hermit and the unceasing toil of a galley slave', what alone made Robert's life bearable

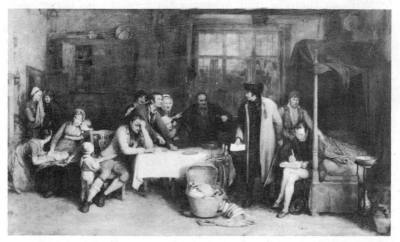

'It's hard to thole the factor's snash'

was the discovery that he could write poetry. A local lad had written a love poem. Not to be outdone, Robert produced his first song, 'My Handsome Nell', for the little village girl who was helping them with the reaping. Though not exactly a work of genius, it has one or two bright flashes, as

'She dresses aye sae clean and neat,
Both decent and genteel;
But there's something in her gait
Gars ony dress look weel.'

It is interesting to see that, at fourteen, he had already decided to write his poetry in the Scottish dialect. His letters show that he could write English very well, but he loved the richness of the Scottish tongue. A fire had now been lit that was to burn in his bosom for the rest of his life.

According to an old Scottish proverb, the income of a farm should be divided into three parts:

'Ane to gnaw, ane to saw,
And ane to pay the laird witha'.'

(One to be eaten, one for running the farm, and one for rent.)

William thought that a bigger farm might be better, and rented one double the size at Lochlea, near Tarbolton. Robert was sent to study surveying and farming mathematics, so that he could lay out the farm for the various crops. As Tarbolton was a village of linen weavers, it was decided to grow flax, the plant from which linen thread is made. Robert was therefore sent to Irvine to study lint dressing, the preparing of the fibre for spinning. This was a long and tedious process, needing great care at every step. The stalks were pulled by hand, tied into sheaves, and left to dry in the sun. Then the seeds were stripped off—they were later crushed to produce linseed oil—and the stalks were soaked in a 'lint hole' for about ten days to rot. The next step was to spread them on the ground to dry, then beat them with a wooden

English Prose versions of the poems quoted are on page 102.

Lochlea Farm, and a certificate showing the amount of corn in stock

knife until the fibres were free from the woody part. These were teased out with a special comb, and sent to the 'lint mill' for spinning into linen yarn. There were about 250 such mills in Scotland, twenty-two of them in Ayrshire.

For four years the family lived quite well on the profits of Lochlea. Then everything began to go wrong. The years of worry, overwork, and under-nourishment had made William grow old too quickly. As his strength failed he became ill-tempered. A quarrel with his landlord ended in long and expensive law suits. William accused the landlord of not draining the land as he had promised, and the landlord protested that the growing of flax every year was exhausting the ground. When their father died, completely worn out, Robert and Gilbert gave up Lochlea, and rented Mossgiel Farm, near Mauchline.

Mossgiel Farm

But though Robert was an expert in farming science, that was not enough. Money was needed, and the brothers had only £7 each, one year's wages from Lochlea. The ground was so high that the frost came early, and stayed well into spring. Sowing was late, and the crops did not ripen in time. As Gilbert wrote later, 'Notwithstanding our utmost diligence and economy, we found ourselves obliged to give up our bargain.'

The failure of Mossgiel made Robert very bitter. As far as he could see, the only people who lived well were the landlords. He put all his resentment into his poems—in the 'Epistle to Davie', for example:

> 'It's hardly in a body's pow'r
> To keep at times frae being sour,
> To see how things are shared.'

or, again, in 'The Twa Dogs', when the Newfoundland says
to the Collie,

> 'Our laird gets in his racked rents,
> His coal, his kane, an' a' his stents.
> He rises when he likes himsel;
> His flunkies answer at the bell;
> He ca's his coach, he ca's his horse;
> He draws a bonny silken purse,
> As lang's my tail, where, through the steeks
> The yellow-lettered Geordie keeks.'

and the Collie replies,

> 'A cottar howkin in a sheugh,
> Wi' dirty stanes biggin a dyke,
> Barin' a quarry, an' sic like,
> Himself, a wife he thus sustains,
> A smytrie o' wee duddy weans,
> An' nought but his han'darg to keep
> Them right and tight in thack and rape.'

Completely disheartened, Robert planned to emigrate to
Jamaica. Meanwhile, hand-written copies of his poems had
been going around, and admiring friends persuaded him to
publish them. In 1786 a slim volume of 'Poems chiefly in the
Scottish Dialect', price three shillings, was produced by a
Kilmarnock printer.

Overnight, Burns was famous. Professors and famous
writers became his friends. A year later a second edition was
published in Edinburgh. This was so well received by the
scholars and aristocrats who thronged the capital, that he
thought no more of emigrating. Instead he went to Edinburgh.

Burns's fame had gone to Edinburgh before him. He was
welcomed into the houses of the grandest ladies and most
famous men. He was the honoured guest at a party given by
the Duchess of Gordon, renowned beauty and wit, favourite
of the King himself. The Earl of Glencairn, President of the

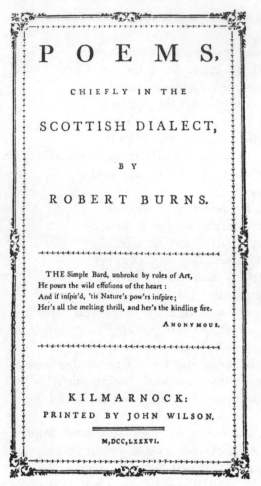

POEMS,

CHIEFLY IN THE

SCOTTISH DIALECT,

BY

ROBERT BURNS.

THE Simple Bard, unbroke by rules of Art,
He pours the wild effusions of the heart :
And if inspir'd, 'tis Nature's pow'rs inspire;
Her's all the melting thrill, and her's the kindling fire.

ANONYMOUS.

KILMARNOCK:
PRINTED BY JOHN WILSON.

M,DCC,LXXXVI.

The title page of the Kilmarnock Edition of the poems

Caledonian Hunt, Edinburgh's most exclusive club, and Henry Erskine, the most brilliant Scottish lawyer, formed lasting friendships with him, and persuaded all their colleagues to order copies of his poems. He was accepted by the playwright John Home, and by Henry Mackenzie, the greatest Scottish novelist of the century, who, in a magazine review of the Kilmarnock poems had called him 'a heaven-born ploughman' and a 'great national poet'.

His brilliant conversation, his wit, his modesty, his dignity, his noble patriotism and his independence, left an impression on all. The Duchess 'had never before met such a man'. A boy at a dinner-party given in the poet's honour by Edinburgh's most brilliant professors wrote many years later that though he had met the most distinguished men of his day he had never seen such 'glowing'

Burns reciting his poems at the Duchess of Gordon's party

eyes as Burns had. The boy was to become famous later as Sir Walter Scott.

Burns was too sensible to allow his head to be turned by all this attention. He had an unusual ability to see people as they really were, and he knew that for many of them he was

The meeting of Burns and Scott

just a nine days' wonder. It was the novelty of being a plough-man poet that made him interesting to them. In a letter to 'The Noblemen and Gentlemen of the Caledonian Hunt', printed at the beginning of the Edinburgh edition of his poems, there was no fawning:

'I was bred to the plough, and am independent. I come to claim the common Scottish name with you, my illustrious countrymen; to tell the world that I glory in the title . . . May tyranny in the ruler and LICENTIOUSNESS in the people equally find in you an INEXORABLE foe'.

Burns sorely regretted that the men who had most inspired his thought and poetry had died shortly before he went to Edinburgh. He made a pilgrimage to the close where Allan Ramsay had had his lending library, the first in Scotland, and had written his 'Tea-table Miscellany' of Scottish songs. He ordered a handsome tombstone to mark the resting place of Robert Fergusson who, dying neglected and in poverty, had yet left behind him his vivid and witty poems of Scottish life that had formed a model for some of Burns's finest poems. In the same Canongate Churchyard lay David Hume, the greatest historian and thinker of eighteenth-century Scotland, whose writings had played a large part in making the Church more gentle towards disbelievers and sinners.

Burns hoped that his Edinburgh friends would find him a well paid job in a government department, so that he might give up farming. Most of all he relied on Patrick Miller, brother of the Lord Justice. A very wealthy man, banker, merchant, owner of coal mines, and chairman of a steelworks, Miller had just bought an estate in Dumfriesshire, and offered the lease of a farm, Ellisland, to Robert. Burns did not want to lose his friendship—and the prospect of a good job—by an outright refusal. Yet his common sense told him that, as a business man, Miller was looking to his own profit first. When he inspected the farm he was sure that the soil was poor. He called in an expert farmer, an old friend of his father, to report on its condition to Mr Miller, convinced that he would advise him against it. To his surprise, the report was favourable. No longer able to refuse, lest he offend Miller, against his better judgment Burns became the tenant of Ellisland Farm.

Three months later he wrote to Gilbert, 'This farm has undone the enjoyment of myself. It is a ruinous affair.' 'Soil!' he said angrily to a friend, 'There never was such soil. God has riddled the whole creation, and flung the riddlings on Ellisland.'

The appointment to a post as Customs and Excise Officer did come, but in a junior grade at £70 a year it was less than he had expected. After three and half years, and the loss of £300 that he had made from the Edinburgh edition of his poems, he gave up farming for ever, and moved with his wife and family to a small house in Dumfries.

An excise permit signed by Burns

2 The Farming System

Why was it that farmers like William Burns and his sons found it impossible to make a living? They worked hard, ate sparingly, yet were always on 'poortith's brink', the edge of poverty. William was one of the finest farmers in Ayrshire. His sons were given a good training, and every opportunity to study farming science. Robert could justly claim, 'At the plough, scythe or reap-hook, I feared no competitor.' He could turn over in one day twice as much as the average ploughman. Their landlords had such confidence in their ability that they had pleaded with them to become their tenants. Yet Mount Oliphant, Mossgiel and Ellisland had been a succession of heartbreaks, and it was only the flax crop that had helped them out at Lochlea. Obviously it was the farming system that was at fault.

Seldom had a land been so sorely neglected. On every side stretched miles of bracken and heather-covered moorland. Constant cropping of oats and barley had sucked the nourishment out of the soil, and there was never enough manure to restore it to health. The original trees had long since been cut down—for houses, ships, fuel, or export to Ireland—and there was no protection against the winds that tore across the moors, no shelter against the frost. The farms crept higher up the hillsides where the land was cold and stony, and the frost lasted long after the seed had been sown, returning before the crop was ripe.

Farming methods were primitive. In one or two counties, it is true, lairds who had travelled to England or Holland returned with zeal for the new farming they had seen there. But, as is usual, most preferred to carry on as their fathers had done before them. They held on as long as possible to the ancient 'infield-outfield run-rig' system.

Around the cluster of farm houses was the *infield*. Beyond that, about six times larger, was the *outfield*. The main crops were grown on the infield. It was divided into strips or 'rigs' of about half an acre, that ran in the shape of an 'S' round the curves of the hills. It was easier to plough that way. The rigs, about twenty feet wide on the crest, sloped outward on both sides to broad marshy ditches. From these spread a luxuriant crop of weeds. Similarly, because they were God's own creatures, flocks of birds were allowed to feed unchallenged on the new-sown seed. New methods and machines were frowned on, particularly the winnowing machine that used 'the devil's wind' to separate the seed from the chaff.

The tenants had a number of rigs according to the rent they paid. To make sure that each received a fair share of good land and bad, these were usually changed by lot each year. The little manure they had was dug in to each third rig in turn, and sometimes the old thatch was added for good measure.

Year about they grew oats and barley. Oats was the main food crop, but was of poor quality, and the normal return was three seeds for each one sown. Today it is about fifteen. In his dictionary Dr Johnson sneeringly defined oats as 'a grain which in England is generally given to horses, but in Scotland supports the people'. Barley, though it provided some of the food, was mainly used for brewing ale, and it, too, was of an inferior type known as 'bear'. Sometimes a little flax was grown to supply the fibre for the coarse linen sarks, or shirts. Some more progressive farmers, like Burns at Lochlea, grew the flax as a crop to sell.

The outfield was rarely manured. It was the pastureland, though bits of it might be ploughed and sown with oats. In the north the cattle were the shaggy black type, ancestors of the modern Highland breed. These were not uncommon in the Lowlands, too, though there the breeding of Ayrshires

15

and Galloways had begun. Beside them browsed the sheep, sorry-looking beasts, about a quarter of the weight of their descendants of today. In the Highlands they were reared both for their milk and for their wool, but the latter was so scanty that it was usually just pulled off by hand, and half a pound per sheep was a normal yield.

As there was little winter feeding, all the cattle and sheep that were not necessary for breeding were sold for slaughtering. The meat was pickled in brine for winter food, but by the turn of the year the flesh was covered with maggots. It still had to be eaten, however. By the 'lifting' time, when the grass had begun to sprout, the surviving animals were so starved that they had to be held steady on their feet and hand fed until they were able to walk again.

Ayrshire was one area where the infield-outfield system was dying out. The farms rented by the Burns family were 'enclosed', that is to say, surrounded by hedges, and occupied by one tenant. To be successful, such a farm needed a lòt of money spent on it. The marshland had to be drained; lime had to be bought to sweeten the soil, fertiliser to feed it, and seeds for the new-type crops—hay, clover, turnips and potatoes. Thousands of young trees had to be planted. The new machines, iron plough, harrow, thresher, winnower, carts, and so on, were very expensive.

The old plough was a clumsy wooden affair that barely scratched the soil. It might be drawn by four horses—'four brutes of gallant mettle', as Burns described them—or eight, ten, or even a dozen oxen ('Owsen frae the furrowed field return sae douf and weary, O'). If there was a shortage of straw, the plough was tied to the animals' tails. It needed a team of at least four men: one to guide it; the driver, who walked backwards in front of the beasts, holding a cross on which the reins were entwined; one right in front to clear away the boulders; one at the side to goad the animals into

16

A twelve-oxen plough

action; and it was as well, if there were enough tenants, to have one or two walking behind to break the clods and level the furrow. With all these men working so hard, they would be lucky to plough half an acre a day.

In the Highlands practically everything was carried in wicker baskets called creels perched high on the backs of the women, or on the flanks of ponies. In the Lowlands sacks were more common, pulled often on sleds tied to the horses' tails. Carts were about the size of modern wheelbarrows, light enough to be lifted out of ruts or ditches. The wheels, made of three bits of wood nailed together, were about eighteen inches in diameter, and revolved with the axle-trees. The first cart with hub and spokes was used in 1723 to carry a small load of coal from East Kilbride to Cambuslang, and crowds turned out to see 'this wonderful machine'. By the middle of the century a few were in use in the Lowlands, none at all in the Highlands.

Changes in Farming Methods, 1750 to 1800
Between 1750 and 1800 great changes were taking place in farming methods and people's lives. The old system was being

17

overthrown so completely that it is usual to say that an 'Agricultural Revolution' took place. Such 'enclosures' as we have already seen in Ayrshire were now to be found throughout the Lowlands and in many parts of the Highlands. Trim-fenced or thorn-hedged fields were taking the place of the rigs. The sheep and cattle were bigger and healthier. As new houses went up they were better built, of stone, though thatching was still not uncommon. The dunghills were further away from them. There were free-standing byres for the cattle, and barns for the grain. Marshes were being drained. Clumps of trees broke the wind—and the monotony. In some areas new forests of fir, larch, oak and beech stretched for miles over the horizon. The people on the whole looked healthier and were better clad, though there were still multitudes of beggars, and many a ruined hut showed where poorer farmers had left the land. Towns and villages were beginning to be linked by well metalled roads. At long last the new farming that had proven so successful in England and Holland was coming to Scotland.

Enclosure of the Ploughland

We have used the word 'enclosure' for the gathering of rigs into compact farms. The word had other meanings too: forming large sheep farms, as in the Highlands; or a single owner taking over pasture that had always been looked on as belonging to the whole neighbourhood. It might mean, too, a large landowner making the woods part of his estate; but there were few woods in Scotland to enclose.

For the ground to produce all the food that it could, the first kind of enclosure was really necessary. The run-rig system was very wasteful. Too much time was spent travelling from one strip to another, perhaps a mile away, or waiting for lazy tenants to turn up so that teamwork could begin. There was always the problem of weeds from the *balks*, or from

a careless neighbour's rigs. We now know that one essential
of good farming is the varying of crops over a period of years,
but there was no possibility of doing that in the run-rig
system.

But although enclosure made better farming, it was often
a tragedy for the small tenant farmer who was pushed out
by the large farmer. We read of fifteen families disappearing
in the village of Crawford, leaving only ruins where they had
lived. In Cadder, 'the parish is now a wilderness . . . The
decent families have been reduced to poverty and scattered.'
In East Kilbride, 'The upper part of the parish was greatly
depopulated by the gathering of small farms into large ones.'
And so it was throughout the land.

Those with money to invest in 'improvement', as the
changes were called, rented large farms and prospered. But
the really poor people suffered greatly.

The New Farming

When ploughland was enclosed the first thing to do was

A winnowing machine

19

to level the rigs. Then the marshland was drained, and the soil was limed and well manured. The iron swing plough that replaced the wooden one needed fewer men and only two horses, and did the work far better than the old one. For the sowing of turnips for winter feeding for the cattle there was the new drill invented by the Englishman Jethro Tull; but for the sowing of grain crops the old wasteful method of scattering the seed in handfuls from a basket strapped round the waist was still used, a feast for the birds that swarmed around. The new-type harrow spread the seed evenly, and covered it with just the right amount of soil. Instead of sickles or pulling by hand, reaping was done by scythes. The threshing machine invented by James Meikle replaced the flail. The fanner, scorned for half a century, now came into its own for winnowing.

There was a tremendous improvement in the quality and quantity of oats and barley. Potatoes, despised for the past

A threshing machine—of an improved type used a few years after Burns's death

fifty years, became the mainstay of many a family, particularly in winter time. Turnips were no longer delicacies that took their place in the fruit bowl with apples and pears. With the new grasses and clover introduced from Holland they provided winter feeding for cattle. The beasts became so much bigger that, we are told, the folk were *scunnered* to look at them. But the milk yield was six times greater, and there was plenty of beef for the market. Great care was taken with the breeding of both cattle and sheep, and they soon began to look like the well-rounded beasts on our farms today. Burns was very proud of his Ayrshire cattle. When he took over Ellisland he was the first to introduce that breed into Nithsdale. He was interested in the breeding of sheep. Mailie, his pet ewe,

> '. . . was nae get o' moorland tips
> Wi' tauted ket, an' hairy hips;
> For her forbears were brought in ships
> Frae yont the Tweed.'

From trial and error it was discovered what crops and treatment best suited the soil and climate. One of the lessons learned was that the sowing of oats and barley year after year sucked the nourishment out of the soil. Healthy abundant crops were possible only on a scientific *rotation*, by which each crop would put into the ground the nourishment the previous one had taken out. The general pattern was that a grain crop, such as oats or barley, should be followed by a root crop, such as turnips or potatoes, with at times a sowing of clover or hay in between. In anything from the fifth to the seventh year the land should be fallow—that is, be allowed to rest and grow its natural grass. On a large farm several different rotations could be going on at the same time, and so all the crops could be grown in any one year.

Burns was well aware of the need for improvement in farming methods. In a letter to his cousin in Montrose he

21

wrote, 'Farming is at a very low ebb with us. We are much at a loss for want of proper methods in our improvements of farming; necessity compels us to leave our old schemes, and few of us have opportunities of being well-informed in the new.' He was one of the few who were well-informed. He spent as much money as he had in fencing the land, draining the bogs, liming the soil, and planting trees. Though he knew the secret of successful farming, he had not enough money to let him wait for the result of his efforts.

Life for the wealthy farmer was good. He had the money to spend on all these improvements, and could enjoy the satisfaction of seeing his land yield more and more. For the poor farmer life was a bitter disappointment: however hard he struggled he could not make enough money to improve his land and get a better living from it.

The Loss of the Common Lands

From the earliest days every town and village had its 'common lands'. Every man—farmer, carpenter, mason, weaver, tailor, shoemaker—could pasture his beasts there, grow some grain, and cut peats for his fire.

Even in Glasgow the town herd set off every morning from his home in the Rottenrow, blowing his cow-horn to warn the citizens to put out their beasts. Down the High Street the cows would straggle, into Trongate, past the Ramshorn Meadow, up Cow Lane, and along Crackling House Brae to the common pasture in Cowcaddens.

For some years past, by private Acts of Parliament, Councils in various towns had been allowed to rent out or sell part of the commons. With the interest in 'improvement', merchants and landowners, who were themselves the members of the Councils, parcelled out the common lands among themselves at ridiculously low prices. In this way Edinburgh, Glasgow, Stirling, Perth, and a host of other towns, lost their

22

common lands in the eighteenth century.

A typical example was the selling by public auction of the lands of Alloway. One of the buyers was Provost Ferguson of Ayr, from whom William Burns was soon to rent Mount Oliphant. Another was a local laird, Robert Hamilton, who bought 600 acres for less than £2,000, and whose son let Mossgiel farm to Robert Burns.

The workers at the trades lost valuable rights in the common lands, and had to depend entirely on their jobs for a livelihood. That was not easy, for the wages were very poor.

The New Rents

The changes we have been describing increased greatly the value of land, so greater rents, in money, were demanded. Some examples will let you see what was happening. In Perthshire land was rented in 1750 at 5s. an acre; in 1795 it was 45s. The increase in the Carse of Gowrie was from 6s. 8d. to £6. In Dumfriesshire in 1760 the total rent paid by farmers was £950. By the time Burns began to farm at Ellisland it was £4,750, a fivefold increase over thirty years.

For the wealthy farmer it was worth while paying the higher rents. The new farming produced heavier crops, of better quality. Cattle, now much sturdier, could survive the winter. The new turnpike roads, providing better and speedier transport, allowed more markets to be reached with the grain, sheep and cattle, mutton and beef, milk, butter, cheese, eggs, turnips, potatoes and vegetables. For the landlords the new rents produced such prosperity as they had never known before.

3 The Highlands

Burns's poems were selling very well. For the first time in his life he had money for a holiday. He made a tour of the borders, and then set off for the Highlands. He travelled, mainly by horse, as far north as ten miles beyond Inverness, and returned by the east coast.

It was like visiting a foreign land. The north and west and the Hebridean Isles were as remote and mysterious to the Lowlanders as darkest Africa was to the explorers of a hundred years ago. The customs of the people seemed as barbarous, and the language they spoke, Gaelic, was as little understood as an African dialect.

The Highlands, wild and primitive, was as far removed in spirit as in distance from the way of life of the south. Its geography, of course, had much to do with this. Each small group of people in its narrow glen was shut off from the next for many months of the year by miles of swampy moorland, roaring torrents and snow-capped craggy mountains. It was impossible for the ways of the south to reach them. Even the Reformation, when the people of the south became Presbyterian, scarcely affected them, and most were still Roman Catholic or preferred the Episcopal religion with its bishops.

With a high sense of loyalty to their own chiefs, it was only natural that the Highlanders should still look on the Catholic Stuarts as the lawful royal family. They had accepted the rule of William III very unwillingly, and his sharp lesson in the Massacre of Glencoe had left a bitter memory. They were still less willing to recognise the German George I.

In the days when the Scottish parliament had met in Edinburgh its laws had little effect on the life of the Highlanders. Now that the Scottish parliament was joined with the English in far-off London, its effect was even less. When

General Wade

in 1715 the Earl of Mar raised the standard of rebellion the Highland chiefs and their clansmen flocked to join him. Though that rebellion failed, they still hoped for success at a later date. To prevent this the government sent General Wade to command the army in the Highlands. He came to the conclusion that the government forts should be linked up with roads so that troops could be rushed to any *Jacobite* trouble spot. Between 1726 and 1740 his soldiers built 250 miles of military roads and forty stone bridges. These new roads did not—and they were not intended to—help the people to drive their cattle more easily to the markets in the south. There were still vast stretches where there was no

Wade's Bridge at Aberfeldy

road at all.

In 1745 Prince Charles Edward Stuart made a last desperate effort to win back the throne of his ancestors. Support came from the Highlanders, but the Lowlanders were more cautious. After the Union of 1707 their trade with England and her colonies was growing, and they did not wish to be involved in a venture that might destroy their new prosperity.

The near-success of this rebellion—its army reached to within 150 miles of London before it was forced to retreat—caused a panic in the south. The government took action to make sure that it could not happen again. Rebel chiefs were beheaded or exiled, their lands were seized by the king. All weapons had to be given up. The king's law was to extend to every part of the kingdom, and the private courts of the chiefs were made illegal. Highlanders were forbidden to wear

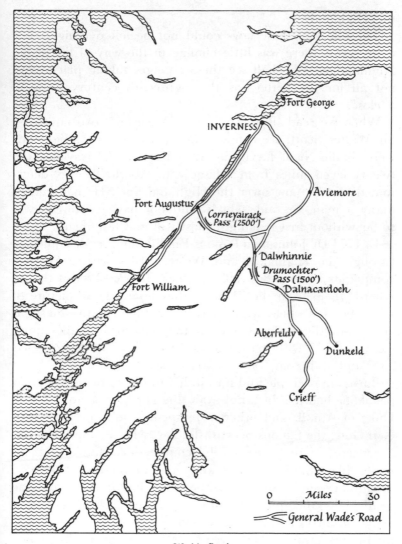

Wade's Roads

their kilts and plaids. Only English was to be taught in schools.
The civilisation of the south, in short, was to be brought to

the Highlands.

The effect of these laws could not be felt overnight. For many years there was little change in the way of life of the Highlanders. We shall see these changes taking place—and not all for the better—as the eighteenth century drew to a close.

When we read 'Rob Roy' and 'Waverley', two novels by Sir Walter Scott, we can see how backward the Highlands were. Bailie Nicol Jarvie, in 'Rob Roy', as he travelled the twenty-seven miles from Glasgow to Aberfoyle, was determined 'not to gang ower the Highland line'. He had known many a man, he said, who would not have ventured even so far without first making his last will and testament.

In 1773 Dr Johnson, a famous Englishman, made a journey through the Highlands and Western Isles with a Scottish companion, James Boswell. In their 'Journals'—you should borrow them from the library—they give a good picture of what they saw. They were horrified by the primitive inns and houses and the stark poverty—of the man, for example, 'quite like a savage', with 'bare legs and feet, a dirty kilt, a ragged coat and waistcoat, (and) a bare head'.

Burns enjoyed splendid hospitality in the castles of the great people he had met in Edinburgh, the Duchess of Gordon, the Duke of Atholl, and others. He spent a jolly evening with Neil Gow, the famous Scottish fiddler, who, like himself, was a collector of the songs of the countryside. But he did not really like the Highlands and its inhabitants. The wild mountain scenery did not appeal to him; he preferred the gentle hills and quiet streams of Ayrshire. He described it as 'a country where savage streams tumble over savage mountains, thinly overspread with savage flocks which starvingly support as savage inhabitants'.

When Burns reached Inveraray the Duke of Argyll was holding a party for his friends in his new castle. The local inn was so crowded that the landlord had no time for an unexpected guest. The poet's pride was hurt, and he put his anger into eight lines of verse:

> 'Whoe'er he be that sojourns here,
>   I pity much his case,
> Unless he come to wait upon
>   The Lord their God—his Grace.
>
> There's naething here but Highland pride,
>   And Highland scab and hunger;
> If Providence has sent me here,
>   'Twas surely in an anger.'

The Clan System
The Clan System had much to do with the primitive wildness of the Highlands. Members of a clan claimed descent from the founder of the tribe in the distant past. A glance at the map on page 30 will let you see where the main clans dwelt.

Some of the chiefs were powerful noblemen. The Dukes of Argyll, Huntly and Sutherland were the chiefs respectively of the Campbell, Gordon and Ross clans; the Earls of Mar and Seaforth and Lord Lovat, of the Macduffs, Mackenzies and Frazers. The majority, however, were poorer and of more lowly station. Each, nevertheless, had unchallenged sway in his own glens. Every clansman owed, and willingly gave, allegiance to him. In return it was the chief's duty to protect his clan, and to keep them from starvation in times of famine.

The chiefs had the right of 'pit and gallows' over their clansmen. That meant that they could fine, imprison, or even sentence to death any of their subjects. Though this right was supposed to be taken away from them after the defeat of the Jacobites at Culloden, they went on punishing people in their own way for many years.

1 Campbell	7 Keppoch
2 Chisholm	8 MacAulay
3 Colquhoun	9 MacFarlane
4 Glassary	10 MacLachlan
5 Glencoe	11 MacLeod of Dunvegan
6 Glengarry	12 Menzies

Map of the Scottish clans

Around his castle or fortress was the *mensal*, the chief's estate. The rest of his land was parcelled out to his nearest kinsmen on *tack* or lease. The tacksmen usually held on to about fifty acres and pastureland for a hundred cattle and the same number of sheep, and divided the remainder among half a dozen tenants. These in turn might let out parts to sub-tenants, and these again might grant an acre or two to a *crofter* who would help him with his farm, or part of an acre to a servant or *cottar*. They all shared the pasture of the outfield. Any one of them, even the tacksman, could be turned off the land at a moment's notice if he did not supply the services demanded as rent, or if the chief had another use for his few acres.

The services were varied and burdensome. Grain, poultry, eggs, ale, and an occasional cow or sheep had to be given. The meal had to be ground at the chief's mill, a part being handed over for the privilege. It was the tenant's job to cut, carry and stack the peats for the chief's fires. He had to help with the ploughing, sowing, reaping and threshing on the mensal. He had to provide the wool for the clothes of the chief's family. In addition he had to pay a small money rent from the sale of a cow or two. Sometimes chiefs asked for quite unreasonable things. The Earl of Seaforth insisted on tongue every day he was in residence in his castle, so that his tenants had to slaughter all their beasts to satisfy his appetite.

The most important service of all was as a soldier in the chief's army. The chief was the warlord, his tacksmen were his officers, the tenants his soldiers, and the cottars the camp

followers. Each clansman had his basket-hilted *claymore*, his *dirk* and *targe*—a shield of oak covered with brass-studded leather, with a spike in the middle. His plaid, of undyed white or grey or moor-red wool, woven in a check pattern (the many-coloured tartan is of much more recent origin) formed his tunic and kilt, and served as a blanket when he

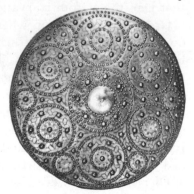

A highland shield, or targe

The Duke of Gordon's sporran

slept on the open moor. In his sporran he had his snuff and tobacco, and perhaps a horn of whisky as well. At his side hung a bag of oatmeal to eat on the campaign.

When the fiery cross went round, the clansman armed himself and set off for the meeting place. The preparation of the cross was a solemn rite. An eighteen-inch cross of yew was set alight, then the flame was quenched in the blood of a newly sacrificed goat. Prayers were offered for success in battle, and a dreadful curse was invoked on any who did not answer the call. The speediest young clansmen carried it aloft in relays through the glens and over the hills. But none refused to call to battle, for the land could not provide a living for even half of the population, and from the *forays* came the plunder that kept them from starvation.

Great was the terror when the bearded clansmen swept down on the Lowland farms. A whole herd of cattle might be driven back to the hills. The farmers were forced to pay 'blackmail', or protection money, to one chief who in return would ensure that no other clan would rob them.

Clans were in a constant state of war with one another, and raids into neighbouring glens were an everyday occurrence. It was to '*extirpate* that band of thieves' that the Campbells had welcomed the opportunity to massacre the Macdonalds of Glencoe. There were also religious reasons, as in this case, too, when one clan was Protestant, and the other Roman

Highland officer and soldier

Catholic or Episcopalian. Or the quarrel might be about clan boundaries, a disputed chieftainship, or because of a *vendetta* arising out of an old act of treachery or murder.

And so the chief could count his wealth in the number of his men, as well as they the food they brought and the chores and the few shillings paid as rent. The Chief of Keppoch calculated his rent roll as five hundred men. The Chief of Barrisdale boasted of £500 a year from blackmail. Rob Roy, the best known of Highland *reivers*, kept his clan well fed on the proceeds of raids and blackmail.

We talk today of brawny Highlanders, and think of power-
fully built men tossing the caber at the Cowal or Braemar
Games. Such a description would not have fitted them in the
eighteenth century. General Wade thought the clansmen thin
and stunted compared with his own Redcoats. One traveller
commented on the women's 'haggard looks, meagre complexions, and bodies weakened by fatigue'. Famine came
often.

The poverty was appalling. It was practically impossible
to grow enough oats, for the farms were too small, the soil
was too poor, and the farming methods were too primitive.
Usually, instead of a plough the *cascrom* was used. This was
a wooden spade tipped with iron. The blade was about two
feet long, and attached at an angle to a six-foot shaft cut
from the branch of a tree. A peg jutted out between the blade
and the shaft. The workman plunged the blade into the
ground, forced it down with the weight of his foot on the

The cas-crom, or foot plough

34

peg, and with a sharp twist raised the clod to the left. About a month's hard work was needed to turn over an acre.

If the family were not to starve some meal would have to be bought. But where was the money to come from? The sale of two cows might fetch £4. Since poor farmers could not afford to drive their own beasts a hundred miles or so to market, the chief would send them with his own in return for a commission. In the markets in Fort William or Inverness or Falkirk some of the money left after the chief had taken his share would go on the purchase of iron to tip the spade, or a brewing vat, or wire for weaving pladding, or needles to sew it with, or a bit of leather—for, with the shortage of trees there was no bark for tanning the hides of their own beasts—or salt for pickling, if they were fortunate to have a cow or sheep to slaughter for winter meat. There was little left for a bag of meal, and what little food was bought had to be looked after with miserly care.

In some coastal areas there was a little fishing—very little. There was no sense in catching more than could be immediately eaten, for there was no market for their surplus. In the Western Isles shellfish were an excellent standby when the grain failed to ripen.

Highlanders had a bad reputation in the south. The adjectives one comes across most frequently are, 'lazy', 'indolent', 'slothful', and 'dirty' and 'unkempt'. Much of this was unfortunately true. A soldier first and foremost, the clansman despised hard work. It was enough if he ploughed and sowed his land. The women could do the rest. It was the women who dug the peats, dried them, and carried them in creels on their backs across the moor for stacking. They did the reaping. They drove the cattle to the sheiling for fattening. They did the milking and made the butter, sometimes putting a live toad in the churn to agitate the thin milk until tiny lumps were formed, and these were held together by a few hairs pulled from the cow's back.

If the Lowland houses were small, crude and dirty, those in the Highlands were many times worse. In some areas the walls were so low that the occupants had to crawl through the door on their hands and knees. Roofs were made of turf, and it was not uncommon to see sheep grazing on them. These were the 'black' houses. Occasionally there would be a 'white' house, the stone-built slated home of a tacksman or laird. At times, more commonly in the Western Isles, the walls would be of two layers of stone about three feet apart,

A village of black houses—The chimneys are later additions

the space between being filled with soil or rubble.

Split logs resting on stones or banks of turf served as seats. Beds were heaps of heather or broom. The floor was bare earth, covered in wet weather with turf from door to bedside. The milk tub, the churn, the wooden bowls and platters, and even the people themselves, were seldom washed.

Breakdown of the Clan System

Highland chiefs became as enthusiastic for enclosure as the Lowland lairds. The clan system was breaking up. Even during the '45 Rebellion there had been signs that the old loyalties were wearing thin. To get recruits some chiefs had ordered the houses of unwilling clansmen to be burned down and their cattle maimed. In one district the men had volunteered when free whisky was provided, but vanished into the night when the supply was finished.

In 1784, the danger of further rebellion being over, the exiled chiefs were allowed to return and buy back their lands. For years they had lived among the nobility in France, Holland or Germany, had served in their armies, and gone to their universities. Those who had not been exiled had spent much of their time in London, and were equally envious of the wealth of the English noblemen. They were all ambitious for more wealth to keep up the standard of living to which they had become accustomed.

The Acts against the clan system were succeeding. If the clansmen did not beat their swords into ploughshares, at least they used their targes to cover the butter churns. Education in English language and English ways was becoming more widespread. As one historian said, the chiefs were no longer the warlords but the landlords. They turned their *henchmen* off the land, tearing the thatch from the roofs, and leaving the walls to moulder away. Even the tacksmen, their nearest blood relatives, were evicted, and Lowlanders with capital and 'know-how' invited to take their place, on long leases and at high rents.

Highland Sheep Farming

Much more devastating for the poorer tenants was the new sheep farming. Early in the 1760s a Ross-shire landowner decided to make his estate more profitable. He drained marshes and planted trees. Then he looked around for a breed of sheep that would not need to be kept indoors and fed in winter time. He brought a herd of Black Lintons from Perthshire, and, to the astonishment of the peasants, they survived the severe winter on the hills, The story of sheep farming in the Highlands had begun.

Soon after, a Caithness laird brought sheep from the Cheviot Hills. No less hardy, they were a third heavier than the native breed, and produced a third more wool. Before the end of the century hundreds of thousands of Cheviots were pasturing on the Highland hills, with as many as 50,000 on a single farm. 'When I was young,' said an aged Highlander, 'the only question asked was, How many men lived on his estate? Then it was, How many black cattle would it keep? But now it is, How many sheep will it carry?'

Three hundred years earlier an English statesman had complained that 'the sheep ate up the people'. This was no less true now in the Highlands. Many thousands of peasants were forced to leave their homes to make way for sheep. Between 1772 and 1792 sixteen vessels full of poor people turned off their land sailed from the western parts of Inverness and Ross to America. An English traveller saw hordes of them 'in a state of desperation, too poor to pay, sell themselves for their passage'. On arrival at the American plantations they were sold as part of the ships' cargoes.

The wars in Europe, India and America provided an outlet for some of the younger men. Many famous Highland regiments were formed, including the Highland Light Infantry and the Seaforths, and many a Scots soldier became famous, though countless more found early graves thousands of miles from home. As early as 1766 the Prime Minister, William Pitt, could boast to the House of Commons that he was the first to bring 'this hardy and intrepid race of men' into the British army, and, he added, 'they served with fidelity, as they fought with valour, and conquered for you in every part of the world'.

Swarms of destitute Highlanders made for the Lowlands. Some went to Edinburgh, where they became town guards,

A sedan chairman

swaggering along the High Street with their great Lochaber axes. Some became *sedan* chairmen, like Edmund Burke, who died penniless, though, as the personal servant of Bonnie Prince Charlie, he could have claimed a £30,000 reward for the betrayal of his master. But most settled in Glasgow and the Clyde region to work in the factories that were springing up. For the women and girls there were jobs as servants in the homes of the rich new factory owners and merchants. So many Highland boys were in distress that the Glasgow Highland Society was formed to try to find work for them. Yet many of these lads were to prosper and become the wealthy tobacco lords.

The 1792 'Rebellion'

Only once, in 1792, did the Highlanders try to drive the 'great sheep' from the hills. Four hundred men from Ross-shire rounded the hated sheep up and drove them southwards. Four regiments were hurried up to stop the 'rebellion'. The peasants ran away in alarm. The sheep were found browsing in a valley near the Cromarty Firth. Ten men were arrested. The Commander-in-Chief of the army wrote to the Home Secretary, 'that no disloyalty or spirit of rebellion . . . was concerned in these tumults, and that they have solely originated in a too well-founded fear that the landed proprietors in Ross-shire and some of the adjacent Highland counties were about to let their estates to sheep farmers, by which means all the former tenants would be ousted and turned adrift.' But as a warning to others, the government dealt very harshly with the men who had been caught. One was transported to Botany Bay in Australia, two were exiled for life, and one was sent to prison until he could pay a fine of £50, which, of course, he could never do. The sheep farmers, with the army and the law helping them, had triumphed, and there was no further serious opposition to their enclosures.

The New Forests

In 1773 Dr Johnson had sneered that 'a tree in Scotland was as rare as a horse in Venice'. It was true, unfortunately, that one could travel many miles from England into Scotland over bare treeless moorland. But had the learned doctor enquired further, he could have been shown many thousands of acres of young saplings, particularly in the north. Not far from his companion James Boswell's estate at Auchinleck William Burns had planted woods and shrubberies in Doonholm. His son Robert did the same at Ellisland.

As early as 1716 at Monymusk in Aberdeenshire the laird had begun planting trees, mainly spruce fir, and before he died there were fifty million on his estate. In 1727 the Duke of Atholl had been given a present of larch plants from the Tyrol, and from these grew twenty-seven million on his own estates, and millions more in the rest of Scotland. When visiting Blair Castle Burns suggested to the Duke that trees should be planted round the beautiful Falls of Bruar. His advice was taken, and within a short time there was a miniature forest on both sides of the stream. Lord Moray planted twelve million oak and elm and beech trees between 1750

Blair Castle, where Burns was entertained by the Duke of Atholl

and 1760, and Lord Findlater eleven million from 1767.

The peasants feared that the roots of the trees would 'suck the heart' out of the soil, and that the birds nesting on them would eat up their seed. It was bad enough, after all, to have to put up with the pigeons from the laird's 'doocot'. Time after time they gathered by night and pulled up the saplings by the roots. But they changed their opinion when it became clear that the trees sheltered the crops from the biting winds, drained the marshes, and provided valuable leaf-mould to feed the soil. We hope they found life more pleasant, too, when the songs of the birds trilled over the countryside.

By 1800 tree planting had become a craze, for the timber was already proving a valuable source of income. The advice offered by a dying laird to his son, in Scott's 'Heart of Midlothian', sums up the new fever: 'Jock, when ye hae naething else to dae, ye may aye be stickin' in a tree; it'll be growing, Jock, when ye are sleepin'.'

Highland Industries

Not all the Highland peasantry wandered south or emigrated. Thousands still lived on tiny patches of land, and, with the increase in rents, were worse off than ever before. In desperation, many moved to the coast to try the fishing or the new *kelp* industry.

Kelp, a chemical made from seaweed, was used in making soap and glass. The weed was cut with sickles, heated in peat-fired stone kilns, cooled, and the ash then sent to the factories in Glasgow and London. Kelp seaweed was found mainly in the Western Isles and the north-west shores of the mainland. A peasant could produce three or four tons a year, and sell it for about £2 10s. a ton. The lairds, however, soon took much of this wealth, for the shore and its seaweed belonged to them. They increased the rent, so that most of the new income went to them, or forced the tenants to sell the kelp to them at a low price, and then re-sold it.

Fishing, too, was now becoming big business. To encourage it the government gave money for the building of big fishing vessels. These *busses*, as they were called, were of about ninety tons, and were built for the Clyde merchants in Greenock, Rothesay and Campbeltown. As the Dutch fishing fleets were scouring the eastern seas, the busses concentrated on the western, and as many as two hundred might be found at a time in a single loch. When the herring were sighted small

A herring buss

boats were lowered, and these loaded their catch into the parent ship. There the fish were salted in barrels, and sent to ports all over northern Europe.

Occasionally small fishermen benefited when busses bought their catch; but more often, as a report pointed out in 1791, it was the habit of the buss crew to 'attack the poor natives of the west coast in their miserable canoes, drive them from their best fishing places, destroy their nets, cruelly maltreat them, and then let down their own tackling'.

If the poor fishermen did have a good catch they often had to dump a lot of it back into the sea, for the salt for preserving it was heavily taxed, and though they could claim back the tax, they could not afford to wait for the money.

White fishing had its problems too. Sometimes the catch had to be sold to the laird at a fixed price. Or he demanded a share, usually every fifth night's catch. Some lairds hired out the boat and tackle, taking half the catch as payment. At Gairloch there was a tax on each fish caught: for each full-sized cod, valued at $2\frac{1}{2}$d., three farthings and 1d. for each ling valued at 4d.'.

In Argyll, Dumbartonshire and the eastern counties women helped out the family income by spinning linen thread. This was winter work, when there was little to do on the farm. Working from sunrise to sunset they could earn $4\frac{1}{2}$d. per day.

4 How the People Lived

Life in the Lowlands in the First Half of the Eighteenth Century
It is difficult for us to realise just how poor the country folk
were at that time. Gilbert wrote of the Lochlea days that
for two years the family tasted no butcher's meat. Robert
resented having to live on 'scarce a bellyful of drummock'—
oatmeal and cold water, without milk. Meal was the main
food of all but the wealthiest. The only variety was in its
preparation. The most common form was porridge: the meal
cooked in boiling water until it was soft and thick, then eaten
with a sup of ale. Kail soup with meal in it was served for
lunch. Another variety was sowans, the meal being stirred
into the water, left to sour for a few days, and eaten cold. For
a change there might be brose, where the water was stirred
into the meal. Instead of bread there were oatmeal bannocks,
or barley bannocks, the latter so tough that a mouthful could
be chewed all day to stave off the pangs of hunger. For a
special visitor, like her daughter's young man in 'The Cotter's
Saturday Night', the thrifty housewife would bring out a bit
of cheese kept specially for such an occasion. At times some
blood was taken from an ox, boiled until it was thick, and
eaten by itself or spread on a bannock. For a real feast, if
an animal died there was haggis, 'Great Chieftain of the
Pudding Race'. The carcase had to be sold; they could not
afford to keep that. But they saved the bits that would go
bad too quickly: liver, kidneys, and intestines. Chopped,
mixed with oatmeal and ox blood, the whole lot was stuffed
into a sheep's stomach, and boiled for hours.

In the paintings of the time you can get a fair idea of the
clothes the people wore. As could be expected, they were
coarse and durable, for most garments were home-made, and
intended to last a long time. The portraits of Burns show him

44

in jerkin and breeches, with a plaid slung over one shoulder, and loosely knotted under the other arm. In cold weather it would be wrapped round him like a cloak. His stockings were of *pladding*, a kind of flannel, and his shoes of tanned leather with very thick soles. He might have a blue Kilmarnock bonnet. His shirt, or 'sark', open at the neck, like Nanny's, in 'Tam O' Shanter', would be of harn—coarse linen—or of pladding. For dress occasions the sark was of finer linen, frilled, and a cravat would be worn round the neck.

For women's clothes look at David Allan's picture of 'A Penny Wedding' (p. 57) and David Wilkie's 'Pitlessie Fair' (p. 55). There they are, in brightly striped woollen dresses, long or short according to whether the wearer is old or young, and attractive *mutches*. For colder weather they had a coat with a hood, of heavy *duffel* cloth. Children and women were usually barefoot, though when going to church or the fair they would carry their shoes, if they were lucky enough to have any, but would not put them on until they got there. In general, children's clothes were a small version of the grown-ups'.

'Miserable hovels' is how the homes of poor tenants and cottars are described by the writer of the following account:

'Many were built in part, and some altogether, of turf, or of mud plastered on stakes and basket work. Clay mixed with straw was used as mortar. The roof was formed of strong *cupples* set up 8 or 10 feet distant from each other, with their feet reaching near to the ground. On these rested cross beams on the sides, and on the top the roof-tree. Some brushwork was laid over the whole, and then *divots* or sods into which oat straw was fixed. The doors were seldom more than 5 feet high; the windows about 18 inches high and a foot wide; the walls from 4 to 5 feet high above the floor. That part that served the family for lodging, sleeping, cooking, dairy, etc., called the inseat, was about twelve or fourteen feet square, with the fire either in the centre or in the gable, without a chimney.

On larger farms another apartment of nearly the same dimensions, and which was entered through the inseat, was called the spense, in which were stored the meal chest, sowen tub, some beds, a cask into which the urine was collected, known by the name of the wash-tub, spinning wheels and reels, and the goodwife's (cheese) press.

The other part of the building was occupied by the cattle.

'A causeway about 6 feet broad was in front of the house. Eight or ten feet beyond that was the dunghill, and beside it the midden-dub, a pond into which the juices of the dung were collected, and dead cats, dogs, etc., were thrown. Sinks and gutters were formed round the house, which received the urine of the cattle, refuse of the dairy, and every offal.'

One can well imagine the stench, both inside and outside the house. It is no wonder that 'if a stranger attempted to approach the house after nightfall, without a guide, he could scarcely avoid sinking to his knees in mire or *putrid* water'.

The floors were just the bare earth trodden hard. If smithy ashes could be had they were spread to form a firmer surface that would not be quite so squelchy when it rained.

The house built by William Burns must have been, in its early days, much like that, for Robert wrote:

> There, lanely by the ingle cheek,
> I sat and eyed the spewing reek,
> That fill'd wi' hoast-provoking smeek
>   The auld clay biggin';
> And heard the restless rattons squeak
>   About the riggin'.

Iron pot and furniture that belonged to Burns—Some of it was better than was usual in a small farmer's house, being bought from his income from his poems

For furniture they seldom had more than a pallet of straw spread in the bed recess, a crude dresser, some shelves arrayed with pewter, wooden, or, occasionally, pottery dishes, a rough bench, a few stools, and one chair reserved for the 'gudeman'.

Dirt and Disease

You could hardly expect people living in such houses to keep clean. 'The clartier the cosier' (The dirtier, the more comfortable) was a common Scottish proverb. People were sewn into their shirts in autumn, and the stitches were not unpicked until spring was well on the way. They washed their faces only before going to church on Sunday. Fleas, bed-bugs and rats were their constant companions.

It is not surprising that there was a great deal of disease. The itch, a nasty skin trouble, was the commonest complaint. Rheumatism, 'when banes are crazed, and bluid is thin', crippled most of the population. Many people died of cholera and typhoid. Smallpox, dyphtheria and 'consumption' took off old and young.

The remedies were often more deadly than the diseases. A famous Edinburgh doctor prescribed as a cure for epilepsy a mixture of pigeons' dung, charred bark of oak, rosemary tops, and white French wine; after this had been strained, powder of human skulls, shavings of elks' hooves, amber and castor were added. Crushed toad was another popular medicine. The list of drugs in a medical textbook published in Edinburgh in 1737 included, in addition to those already mentioned, the juice of woodlice; spiders' webs; frog spawn; ants' eggs; human blood, fat and urine; mummy scrapings; excrement of horse, pig, peacock and goat; mother-of-pearl; and a great deal more. If all these failed, the next course was to open an artery, and draw off a cupful of blood. In 'Death and Dr Hornbook' Burns poked somewhat cruel fun at the schoolmaster, who eked out his living by acting as local medical adviser and chemist. The poet claimed that when he was walking in the moonlight he met the spectre of Death, with his scythe over his shoulder. The ghost was in a most miserable state, and complained bitterly that 'Hornbook', with his cures, was putting him out of business, causing more people to leave this world than Death ever did.

The Beggars

As soon as she was married a woman began to spin the wool for the family's *winding sheets,* and her husband tried to

A beggar, or blue gown—note the permit badge pinned to his coat

put by a few shillings for the funeral expenses. No shame was greater than to be buried in a pauper's grave. Yet, for one in every ten, this was the final disgrace.

'The last o't, the warst o't,
Is only but to beg.'

So wrote Burns. The land was swarming with beggars. Parish officers issued permits for begging, and supplied blue gowns as a kind of uniform. The 'Blue Gowns', as the beggars were called, were given regular beats. No one, no matter how poor, refused to put a handful of meal into their 'pokes', or 'gaberlunzies', as their wallets were called. A collection for the parish poor was taken in church every Sunday, but there was seldom more than a shilling or two in the plate.

While the law was sympathetic to the 'deserving' poor, there were other types of beggars that it dealt with very sternly. These were the *sorners*, gypsies and tinkers, to name only a few. They swarmed across the moors in bands, terrifying the peasants in lonely farmhouses. They turned up at weddings, christenings and funerals to claim a share of the leftovers. They were notorious thieves, responsible for many a murder, maiming and kidnapping. For the sorners, those who extorted money or food by threats, the penalty was banishment for the first conviction, and hanging if they returned. For the first offence vagabonds, gypsies and tinkers had a hole burned in their ear, and were sent back to the parish they had come from. They, too, could be hanged if they returned.

In 'The Jolly Beggars' Burns gives a lively picture of these rogues, wild, carefree and defiant, having a gay old time in Poosie Nancy's Inn in Mauchline. The old soldier was there in his 'auld red rags', the remnants of his uniform, with his unpleasant girl friend. He had fought in Canada and Cuba, and at the siege of Gibraltar, but now, with only one arm

Poosie Nancy's Inn, Mauchline

and a wooden leg, was thrown on the scrap heap. His companions were a professional clown, popular once in the homes of the wealthy, but, past his best, no longer able to make a living; a vagabond thief, widow of a hanged Jacobite; a fiddler; a tinker; and, of course, a poet. Though Burns, with his sympathy for all unfortunates, had a fellow-feeling for them, they were, no doubt, a danger to decent-living people.

Country Education

At Alloway, William Burns sent his sons to the village school. When he moved to Mount Oliphant, remembering what his father had done, he persuaded his neighbours to join with him in hiring a teacher, putting him up in turn, at a wage of sixpence a day. The children were lucky, for John Murdoch, the teacher, was an enthusiast who taught them much more than most of the teachers of the day would have done. Besides the Bible and religious books he studied with them the works of Shakespeare and other English and Scottish writers. He borrowed books for them from the libraries of his wealthier friends. He gave a good grounding in English grammar, writing, arithmetic and psalm-singing. Later Robert, his favourite pupil, spent an occasional week with Murdoch in Ayr, and learned some French and Latin.

The schooling lasted only two years. When he was nine, Robert had to do a full day's work on the farm. Then, in the firelight on the winter evenings, his father, lean and gaunt, taught his family some arithmetic, or read in a solemn voice from the Old and New Testaments. Mrs Burns had a sweet voice. As she sang the old airs and ballads of the countryside she gave her son that love of music that was to make him the greatest song-writer of all time.

The Burns children loved the stories told by a poor old widow who helped at times with the milking and spinning. The people of those days were very superstitious, and old

Betty had, as Robert tells us, 'the largest collection in the country of tales and songs concerning devils, ghosts, fairies, brownies, witches, *warlocks*, *spunkies*, *kelpies*, elfcandles, deadlights, *wraiths*, apparitions, *cantraips*, giants, enchanted towers, dragons, and other *trumpery*'. Years later Burns put much of this into his great poems 'Tam O' Shanter' and 'Hallowe'en'.

The ingle of the Tam O' Shanter Inn—now a museum. The figures are of Tam and Souter Johnnie

Though a few were now beginning to know better, most people still believed that every catastrophe was the work of the Devil and his fiendish band. The cure for a fever was to wave the pages of the Bible in front of the patient, and mutter a prayer. The fairies could not steal a new-born baby and put a changeling in its place if the relatives formed a circle round the cradle, and the father waved the 'Good Book' to and fro. A whitlow could be cured by sticking a finger in a cat's ear, and a stye by brushing the eye with a cat's tail. If the fish were not biting, it was because the goddess of the sea was angry. In days of old she would have needed a human sacrifice, but now it was enough to swing a boy over the waves, and pretend to throw him in. At Hallowe'en, which marked the end of the year at that time, the souls of the dead came to warm themselves at the fire, and feed on the cakes and ale provided by thoughtful relatives. Outside, fairies and hobgoblins were waiting, and witches galloped on tabby cats or sped through the air on broomsticks. A bonfire would keep them at bay, and the boys went from house to house in the village begging for peats to burn the witches. Similarly at Beltane, the first of May, to make sure of a good harvest, bonfires were lit, and a sacrifice offered— now only a newly baked cake. From the bonfire new fires were lit in every house to bring new life to the countryside. There were magic wells, magic stones, and magic swords. You were more or less safe if you had a bit of iron, even a nail, in your pocket.

Like the Burns family, many made sacrifices for the education of their children. Yet, despite Acts of Parliament ordering tenants and landlords in every parish to provide a 'commodious house' for a school, and share the cost of the teacher's salary, in 170 parishes in the Highlands, and in many square miles of the Lowlands, there was no school. There might be occasional teaching by some semi-starved semi-illiterate *dominie* who wandered from croft to croft exchanging his smattering of knowledge for a bowl of porridge and a bed of straw. Alarmed at the paganism in the Highlands, the Scottish Society for the Propagation of Christian Knowledge set up a number of schools; but children who understood only Gaelic did not learn much when all the teaching was in English.

Teachers' salaries, even in those days, had been fixed by law. Too often they did not get even the little that they should; tenants and landowners just would not pay their share. The dominies had to make do with the few coppers and the meal sent by parents, eked out by a few shillings earned as session clerks, registrars, or grave-diggers.

As often as not the school was held in a tumbledown byre or in a corner of the teacher's but and ben. We read of the children bringing straw to thatch the roof, but it was so scarce that only half could be covered. The rain poured through the other half. There were sometimes no desks and seats, and the writing was done lying flat on the muddy floor. In winter and bad weather the light was blotted out by the turfs stuffed into the window. The fug of peat smoke did not

A schule scailin'

make studying any easier. Rats, cooking, and the crying of babies were normal distractions.

In summer the school day started at seven. Many a pupil had to set off an hour earlier to trudge across the moor. At six the homeward tramp began. In winter the hours were from sunrise to sunset, for the dominie could not afford the wax candles of the gentry or the evil-smelling tallow ones of the tenantry, but had only the spluttering fitful light of splinters of fir trees whose resin gave off the most pungent fumes. Parents might take children from school for the harvesting, but no absence was allowed on Sundays, for then the teacher marched his charges to a service in the morning, and another in the afternoon, and the rest of the day was taken up with religious instruction.

The Laird's son and the cottar's son sat at the same desk, or squatted side by side on the floor. This may be one reason why Scotland tended to be more democratic than England.

Country Entertainment

Forced to work at such an early age, Robert Burns could have had little time for playing. His father would not have liked it, anyway, for, deeply religious, he had little time for frivolity. Indeed, the first disagreement between them was when Robert joined a dancing class. Yet, despite the long day at lessons, most children had their playtime too. They spun their 'peeries' or tops, flew their kites, played with ball and skipping ropes, pitched quoits, had fun at leap-frog, formed shinty teams, and in winter went curling with their fathers. Instead of Cowboys and Indians they played English and Scotch.

It was an exciting time when the fair was held in the village.

Pitlessie Fair

55

The conjurers were there, and the tumblers, and many queer strangers. There would be a *bawbee* to spare for a fairing—gingerbread or Gibralter rock or Black Man or London candy— sold, as someone complained, 'by creatures labouring under the worst of diseases, and abominably nasty: carried for weeks in their dirty wallets from one beggar-inn to another'. Youths and adults, too, relaxed from toil to enjoy the fair.

There were other occasions when the cares of life were left behind. At the great Communions, when as many as five thousand might come from parishes round about, there was fun when the preaching was over—and, to the horror of the ministers, even during the preaching. Love-making and merry-making took place in the balks nearby. Burns enjoyed himself at these 'Holy Fairs' in Mauchline and

Mauchline Holy Fair

Tarbolton. Other happy occasions were Hallowe'en, when
'Love blinks, wit slaps, an' social mirth
Forgets there's care upo' the earth.'

and Ne'erday, when

> 'The nappy reeks wi' mantlin' ream
> An' sheds a heart-inspiring steam;
> The luntin pipe, the sneeshin mill,
> Are handed round wi' right guid will.'

The highlight of the social round was the 'Penny Wedding'. In a community so poor it had become the custom for the neighbours to give a penny Scots (the twelfth of an English penny) for food and drink for the guests. The name was still used, though the guests now subscribed what they could afford, usually meal, poultry, ale, and even whisky. The fiddles, looked on by the ministers as the deadliest weapons of the Devil, played their merriest reels, and the young folks risked everlasting punishment by dancing together. The older men, always fond of argument and deep discussion, after

A 'Penny Wedding'

'twalpennyworth of nappy' (a shilling's worth, Scots, of ale),

> 'Laid aside their private cares
> To mind the Kirk and State affairs'.

Women had their own social occasions. 'Rocking' was the

The village politicians, talking of 'Kirk and State affairs'

A girl with a rock, or distaff

most popular. 'Rock' was the Scots name for a *distaff*. In earlier days they had come together to gossip while spinning; but now the rocks were left at home, and laughter and singing suggested that the 'gentle dames', too, had their share of nappie.

The Kirk

An account of life in Scotland at this time would not be complete if we did not include the Church, or 'The Kirk', as it was called. The Church of Scotland was 'Presbyterian', so called because it was governed by the decisions of *presbyteries*, or councils of ministers and of elders elected by the congregations.

58

Charles I tried to force the Scottish Church to have bishops and a prayer book on the English model. In 1638 the Scots signed a 'National Covenant' in which they pledged themselves to protect the Church, even with their lives, and defeated the armies that the king sent against them. Soon Charles was at war with his English parliament too, and in 1643 the Scots agreed to help to defeat him on condition that Presbyterianism became the religion of England and Ireland as well as of Scotland. At Westminster English ministers and representatives of the Scottish Church drew up a 'Confession of Faith' in which the Presbyterian beliefs were fully explained.

In less than twenty years the English became tired of Presbyterianism, and when Charles II came to the throne he appointed bishops to the English Church, and ordered the Scots to have bishops too. In the reigns of both Charles II and James II the Scots were severely punished because they would not do so, and these years are known as 'The Killing Times'. Only when William III became king in 1689 were the Scots allowed to worship in their own way. Not surprisingly, the Kirk determined to make sure that everybody was true to the faith for which it had fought so hard and suffered so much. By an Act of the Scottish parliament in 1690 all Scots had to worship according to the Confession of Faith.

The 'Confession' is a long and difficult document to read. But it is important to know what its main points are. As the Bible reveals 'the whole counsel of God', all questions of Christian faith are decided by its words. By eating the forbidden fruit Adam and Eve introduced sin into the world, with death as its consequence. All mankind has inherited their guilt, but can be saved by faith in Christ. To earn this, men must always make the Scriptures their guide, 'sing the psalms with grace in their hearts', and receive the sacraments. There are some, the 'Elect', whom God has chosen for everlasting grace, and from these come the ministers and the elders. Those who have sinned must be punished, but if they become truly penitent they may still find grace; but those who continue to be wicked and ungodly are given over to Satan. On Sunday all must rest from workaday labours, words and thoughts, and spend the whole time in public and private worship and other holy ways. It is the duty of the ministers and elders to deal with the sinners, and bring them to repentance, and mete out the punishments that are necessary.

The Kirk in the eighteenth century took this last duty very seriously, and kept a constant watch over every movement and word of the people. On the Sabbath an elder scoured the parish to make sure that all who were not ill were in church; or, the services over, to see that no misguided soul took a stroll through the meadows, rested in bed, looked out of the window, read a book other than the Bible, or even talked about non-religious subjects. From every home he must hear the singing of psalms, the reading aloud of the Holy Book, or the father questioning his children about the lesson in the sermon.

Offenders were summoned before the *Kirk Session*, the meeting of the ministers and elders of the parish. Usually they were fined, or made to stand in sackcloth on a stool in front of the congregation while the minister delivered a sermon on the punishment that awaited them. This might be repeated for weeks, or even months. Many young women committed suicide rather than face the shame of the Kirk's rebuke. Burns felt that the Kirk was too severe, and that many of the elders were no better than the people they were condemning. This led him to write some of his most bitter poems. He himself had been fined, and shamed on several occasions; but perhaps he deserved his punishment more than most.

Too severe they might be, but the ministers were sincere and goodliving, 'preserving', as one Englishman said, 'within a narrow income a dignity too often lost among their brethren south of the Tweed'. Well might he refer to their 'narrow' incomes, for the ministers were as poor as their parishioners, and as often as not their stipend, as their pay was called, was paid in meal and peats.

Life in the Lowlands in the second half of the Eighteenth Century
As the years went on the nation as a whole became more prosperous because of the better farming methods, new industries, and an increase in trade. Some of the better living was passing to the labouring classes, though many were as poor as ever. Wages in many cases doubled in the second half of the century, but prices also rose sharply. People had more varied food, if not much more plentiful. The reports of the parish ministers give much information about this. Oatmeal and kale are still the main foods, but turnips sometimes take the place of greens, and 'potatoes, dressed in different ways, with butter, milk, onions, etc., are commonly one third of their food from the beginning of September to the middle of March'. But 'the cottagers and the poorer sort of people have not always milk or beer to their meals'. In the small farmer's home things are getting better than they were for the hungry Burns family at Lochlea. 'Formerly there was little beef or mutton used. Even a farmer's family thought themselves sufficiently provided in flesh-meat with an old ewe killed about Christmas. For such a family at present sixteen stones of beef and two good sheep are considered a moderate provision.'

Two *baneful* additions to the diet were deplored by many ministers: tea and whisky.

'Prior to 1745 there was not a tea kettle in the parish except the minister's; now, there is not a farmhouse without one, and several of the sub-tenants use the same piece of furniture.' 'The very poorest classes begin to no inftances of fuicide, nor of any executed or banifhed for capital crimes, in the remembrance of any now living.

As it may doubtlefs prove entertaining to many readers, to obferve the progrefs of manners in the fpace of 30 years, the following comparifon is added, between the ftate of this parifh in 1760 and in 1790, in fundry particulars.

COMPARATIVE STATEMENT *of the parifh in* 1760 *and* 1790.

In 1760, Land was rented at 6 s. an acre, on an average only 2 fmall farms were inclofed.

In 1790, Land is rented at 30 s. an acre, all inclofed with ftone dikes and thorn hedges.

In 1760, No wheat was fown in the parifh, except one half acre by the minifter, no grafs nor turnip feed was fown, and no kail nor potatoes planted in the open fields.

In 1790, Above 100 acres are fown with wheat; about three fifths of the ground are under grafs, turnips, kail, and potatoes.

In 1760, Land was plowed with oxen: only a few horfes were kept to draw the harrow in feed time, and bring in the common harveft. L. 7 was thought a great price for a horfe.

In 1790, Oxen are not employed in agriculture. Farmers have their faddle horfes, worth from L. 24 to L. 30, and work horfes from L. 20 to L. 25 each.

In 1760, The wages of men fervants, that followed the plough, were L. 3 a-year: of maid fervants, L. 1, 10 s.

In 1790, Men fervant's wages are L. 8, fome L. 10 : maid fervant's ditto L. 4.

In 1760, Day labourers were got at 6 d. a-day; tailors at 3 d. wrights at 6 d.; and mafons at 10 d. a-day.

In 1790, Day-labourers receive 1 s.; tailors 8 d. wrights 1 s. 2 d. and mafons 2 s. a-day.

In 1760, No Englifh cloth was worn but by the minifter and a quaker.

In 1790, There are few who do not wear Englifh cloth : Several the beft fuperfine; cotton vefts are common.

In

Two pages from the Statistical Account of Scotland

In 1760, Men's stockings in general were what was called plaiding hose, made of white woollen cloth ; the women wore coarse plaids : not a cloak, nor bonnet, was worn by any woman in the whole parish.

In 1760, There were only two hats in the parish ; the men wore cloth bonnets.

In 1760, There was only one eight day clock in the parish, six watches, and one tea kettle.

In 1760, The people in this parish never visited each other, but at Christmas. The entertainment was broth and beef ; the visitors sent to an alehouse for five or six pints of ale, and were merry over it without any ceremony.

In 1760, Beef and mutton were 2 d. *per* lb.; butter 5 d. *per* lb. ; cheese 2 s. 6 d. *per* stone, and eggs at 1 d. halfpenny *per* dozen.

In 1760, In this parish there were four meal mills, one washing mill for cleaning yarn, one wauk mill, and one snuff mill.

In 1760, There was one bleachfield in the parish, which employed 10 persons.

In 1760, Children at school had a piece of pease bread in their pockets for dinner.

In 1790, Cotton and thread stockings are worn by both sexes, masters and servants ; some have silk ones : the women who wear plaids have them fine, and faced with silk ; silk plaids, cloaks and bonnets are very numerous.

In 1790. Few bonnets are worn ; the bonnet-maker trade in the next parish is given up.

In 1790, There are 30 clocks, above 100 watches, and at least 160 tea-kettles, there being scarce a family but hath one, and many that have two.

In 1790, People visit each other often ; a few neighbours are invited to one house to dinner ; six or seven dishes are set on the table, elegantly dressed ; after dinner a large bowl of rum punch is drunk ; then tea ; again another bowl ; after that supper, and what they call the grace drink.

In 1790, Beef and mutton are 4 d. *per* lb. ; butter 10 d.; cheese 5 s. 4 d. *per* stone, and eggs 6 d. *per* dozen.

In 1790, There are 3 meal mills, 17 washing mills, 5 mills for beating thread and cloth, one wauk mill, one snuff mill, and 5 barley mills.

In 1790, There are 9 bleachfields which employ above 100 persons.

In 1790, Children at school have wheaten bread, sweet milk, butter, cheese, eggs, and sometimes roast meat.

Is

regard it as one of the necessaries of life, and, for its sake, resign the cheaper and more invigorating nourishment that the products of their own country afford.'

Tea, bought from Glasgow or London, was about 4s. a pound, and the sugar to sweeten it about 4½d. a pound. Tea and whisky are often mentioned in the same sentence as equally dangerous.

It was the last straw when they were combined, and the last cup of tea was mixed with a little whisky, which was supposed to correct all the bad effects of the tea. We can imagine the despair of the minister in Lewis who complained that 'maid-servants were in the habit of drinking every morning a wine-glass of whisky, which their mistresses gave them'. The whisky, incidentally, cost 3s. 6d. for a half gallon.

Another habit that was frowned upon was the fondness of the older women for their pipe of tobacco. In Burns's 'Hallowe'en', old Grannie was so annoyed at the youngsters' games that she 'fuff'd her pipe wi' sic a lunt'—puffed with so much smoke—that she didn't notice that a cinder had burned a hole in her apron.

Clothes, too, came in for criticism:

'Formerly the women of inferior stations appeared in church on Sunday in bed-blankets or tartan plaids; but now they wear scarlet plaids or duffle coats and bonnets, and maid-servants are as well dressed as their mistresses. Formerly farmers and respectable tradesmen were contented with the blue bonnet and with *say* for their best clothes, but now, not only farmers and master tradesmen, but farm-servants and apprentices, and cottagers frequently appear at kirk and market in hats and English broadcloth. Formerly clocks and watches were little used in the parish, excepting, perhaps, by the laird or the minister; but now, in general, every farmer has his eight day clock, and almost every servant has his watch.'

Burns, in his Kirkoswald days had been a bit of a dandy. Here is his description of himself:

'His coat is the hue o' the bonnet sae bene,
His fechet as white as the new driven snaw,
His hose they are blae, and his shoon like the slae,
And his clear siller buckles they dazzle us a'.

He had two pairs of blue plush breeches, a ten-shilling hat, a linen cravat, and five snow-white linen shirts. On his father's death he, as the eldest son, inherited his pocket watch.

This next picture is by a traveller who knew the country well: 'Not many years ago the people were wretchedly poor, want sat on every brow, hunger was painted on every face; neither their clothes nor miserable cottages were a sufficient shelter from the cold. You see the ploughman now in church in his coat of blue cloth at 5s. 6d. a yard, velveret vest and corduroy breeches; white cotton stockings, calf-skin shoes; black silk shoulder knots, shirt with ruffles at the breast,

At the spinning wheel

white muslin cravat, fringed; hat worth 8s. to 10s.' The girl friends accompanied him in 'gay ribbons, silks, muslins, and printed cottons of England'.

This was all right when single, but after marriage it was a different story. A labourer's wages averaged about £15 a year in the prosperous areas, while in remote parts, as in the north-west Highlands or the Western Isles, it might be only £2 10s. and four pairs of brogues a year.

Here is the actual budget of a year's income and expenditure of a man with a wife and three children. Even with the barest living, there was nothing to spare, and to make ends meet the wife had to do a good deal of spinning:

INCOME

	£	s.	d.
Man—48 weeks at 6s.	14	8	0
Woman—48 weeks' spinning at 1s. 6d.	3	12	0
	18	0	0

EXPENDITURE

	£	s.	d.
2 pecks oatmeal per week at 11½d.	4	19	8
2 pecks barley or pease meal per week at 7½d.	3	5	0
6 bolls potatoes at 5s. (1 boll=48 lbs.)	1	10	0
barley for kale, 3 lb. a week	0	16	3
kaleyard and wretched house	0	13	0
milk, 4d. per week	0	17	4
salt, cheese and butter	0	12	6
soap for washing clothes	0	2	6
coals and carriage	1	0	0
shoes to the whole family	1	0	0
body clothes to the man	1	10	0
body clothes to the wife and children	1	5	0
worsted thread for mending	0	7	0
	17	18	3

There was no allowance for wages lost through sickness, for medical or funeral expenses, or schooling for the children.

In 'The Cotter's Saturday Night', Burns gave a delight-

6 The Cotter's Saturday night. *Inscribed to R. Aiken, Esq.*

Let not Ambition mock their useful toil,
   Their homely joys, and destiny obscure;
Nor Grandeur hear, with a disdainful smile,
   The short and simple annals of the Poor. *Gray.*

1
My lov'd, my honor'd, much respected friend
   No mercenary Bard his homage pays;
With honest pride, I scorn each selfish end,
   My dearest meed, a friend's esteem and praise:
To you I sing, in simple Scottish lays,
   The lowly train in life's sequester'd scene;
The native feelings strong, the guileless ways,
   What Aiken in a Cottage would have been;
Ah! tho' his worth unknown, far happier there I ween!

2.
November chill blaws loud wi' angry sugh;
   The short'ning winter-day is near a close;
The miry beasts retreating frae the pleugh;
   The black'ning trains o' craws to their repose :
The toil-worn Cotter frae his labor goes,
   This night his weekly moil is at an end,
Collects his spades, his mattocks and his hoes,
   Hoping the morn in ease and rest to spend,
And weary, o'er the muir, his course does hameward bend.

3
At length his lonely Cot appears in view,
   Beneath the shelter of an aged tree;
Th'expectant wee-things, toddlan, stacher thro'
   To meet their Dad, wi' flichterin noise and glee.
His wee-bit ingle, blinkan bonilie,
   His clean hearth-stane, his thrifty Wifie's smile,
The lisping infant, prattling on his knee,
   Does a' his weary kiaugh and care beguile,
And makes him quite forget his labor and his toil.

First page of 'The Cotter's Saturday Night', in Burns's own handwriting

67

fully realistic account of the life of a poor farming family. The ploughman, tired at the end of a week's work, trudges home over the fields on a raw blustery winter's evening:

> November chill blaws loud wi' angry sugh;
> The short'ning winter-day is near a close;
> The miry beasts retreating frae the plough;
> The black'ning trains o' craws to their repose:
> The toil-worn cotter frae his labour goes—
> This night his weekly moil is at an end,
> Collects his spades, his mattocks, and his hoes,
> Hoping the morn in ease and rest to spend,
> And weary, o'er the moor, his course does hameward
> bend.

> At length his lonely cot appears in view,
>   Beneath the shelter of an aged tree;
> Th'expectant wee-things, toddlin, stacher through
>   To meet their dad, wi' flichterin' noise and glee.
>   His wee-bit ingle, blinkin bonilie,
> His clean hearth-stane, his thrifty wifie's smile,
>   The lisping infant, prattling on his knee,
> Does a' his weary kiaugh and care beguile,
> And make him quite forget his labor and his toil.

The older children drop in, having a week-end rest from their jobs as servants or plough hands. They hand over to their parents their hard-won wages. There is a good deal of banter and gossip, mother listening attentively while mending the old clothes. The father gives his family advice on how to behave when away from home:

> 'Their master's and their mistress's command,
>   The younkers a' are warned to obey;
> And mind their labors wi' an eydent hand,
>   And ne'er, tho' out o' sight, to jauk or play;
>   "And O, be sure to fear the Lord alway".'

There's a knock at the door. The eldest daughter's boy-friend pays his first visit to her home. In his honour, when the simple supper of porridge and milk has been served, the mother brings out the little bit of precious cheese that has been stored for such an important occasion. Supper over, they form a wide circle round the fireplace, the father reverently lays aside his bonnet, says grace, and reads aloud from his big Bible. All join in the singing of old Scottish psalms.

That this was a true picture of an evening in the life of a typical Scottish peasant family we know from an amusing story. Burns had sent a copy of the poem to a wealthy old Ayrshire lady. When she went into raptures over it her old servant could not understand what all the fuss was about. 'Nae doubt gentlemen and ladies think muckle o't,' she said, 'but for me it's naething but what I saw in my ain faither's house every night, and I dinna see how he could hae tauld it ony other way.'

We must remember, though, that even at the end of the century there were still too many who, with no work, or too ill or old to work, were in great distress. In report after report the ministers tell of their poverty. In Wick 150 poor people received 2s. a week each; in Dornoch 80 to 100 shared £7 a year; 'so that the poor live by begging from parish to parish'. In addition, there were thousands of 'reduced householders who would rather starve than beg.'

5 The Life of the Gentry

The great lords spent so much of their time in London that their way of living had become more English than Scottish. But, until the middle of the eighteenth century most of the Highland chiefs and Lowland lairds continued to live in much the same way as their better-off tenants. They wore the clothing made by the travelling tailor from the locally woven cloth. Their main foods were meal and kale, and their main drink was ale. Their houses, except that some might have a second storey and a slate roof, were very much of the type that we have already described. The new prosperity brought about a revolution in their way of living. They began to spend lavishly, and in many cases extravagantly.

When Burns grew famous he was invited to many homes of the gentry, and had a chance to study their way of living. He contrasted it with the poverty of his lowly friends and neighbours. The pomp, extravagance and snobbery, and the affected airs of many of his hosts made him exceedingly angry. When he met genuine worth, however, he was the first to praise it. He became very friendly with young Lord Daer, for example, for

'nae pride had he,
Nor sauce, nor state that I could see,
Mair than an honest ploughman.'

He counted the Earl of Glencairn among his intimate friends, and when that nobleman died he wrote a touching elegy. On his Highland holiday he spent delightful days at the castles of the Countess of Gordon and the Duchess of Atholl. The duchess actually tried to bribe the driver of his *chaise* to remove a shoe from his horse so that he might stay with the family for a few days longer. When he poured his scorn on the gentry, as he often did in his poems, we know that he has in mind the many others who disgusted him with their airs and graces.

Turn back to page 9, and read the lines from the poem 'The Twa Dogs'. Here Burns is indignant and sarcastic about the wealthy. They are not really 'ill-hearted fellows', he says, but thoughtless, rather. He is bitter about the racked rents, rents that were put up with every improvement in the farm or farmhouse. For the lairds,

'Frae morn to e'en it's nought but toiling
At baking, roasting, frying, boiling.'

Some 'go a-parliamenting', and eager for power, 'say aye or no' as the Prime Minister directs. To keep up style with their English friends they spend freely on balls and masquerades, visit the theatre, go to the races, and gamble heavily, there, or at cards, 'the Devil's picturebuiks'. They travel all over Europe—to Versailles, Vienna, Calais, Madrid, the Hague— to learn '*bon ton*' and see the world. They drink far too much. They borrow to pay their debts, and have to sell their estates to repay the loans. Their ladies spend their time playing— and cheating—at cards, and over their 'wee bit cup and platie' gossip maliciously and tear reputations to shreds.

Houses

A great deal of building and rebuilding was taking place. Castles had been built for defence in the troubled days of old. That had been more important than comfort. Claypotts Castle, near Broughty Ferry in Angus, is typical of many built from the thirteenth century to the sixteenth. It is a dour structure, with walls many feet thick, and you can easily imagine how dismal, cold, damp, draughty and comfortless it must have been inside. The windows are few and small. The big chimneys sticking out on top from the inside of the walls give a hint of the enormous fires needed to bring any

Claypotts Castle

warmth into the place at all. Below ground level were the dungeons where those unfortunates captured on a raid or condemned under the right of pit and gallows were imprisoned. On the ground floor were the stores, weapons and cattle. Above was the great hall where family, guests and retainers dined, and where the latter slept on straw or heather. Adjoining it was the withdrawing room where the lord would meet his most intimate friends or plan the next campaign. The house, with bedrooms for the family, was on the top floor, the beds being set in recesses in the thick walls.

There might be differences from castle to castle, but some features were common to most. The gable reached right up to the roof ridge, and had a series of steps on the sloping parts—'corbie steps', so called, no doubt, because the corbie, or crow, found them a convenient resting place. The central portion was a solid square structure, the 'keep'. Towers, either round or square, were often added at the ends. A bulge in the wall showed where the narrow spiral staircase wound its way inside. Sticking out from the roof were small *dormer* windows, so called from the French 'dormir', to sleep. Sometimes turrets on the end towers, copied from French castles, remind us of the Auld Alliance; or a projection with a double curve, such as are found in old Dutch buildings, tells of our long trading association with Holland.

With the end of the border wars in the seventeenth century, and the taming of the Highlands in the eighteenth, the need for castles and keeps disappeared. Comfort became more important than defence. The nobles made alterations and additions to the family fortresses, or built new palaces and mansion houses, modelled on the homes that English noblemen had been building in the past hundred years. While sometimes these houses looked Scottish, generally they were in the 'classical' style.

The word 'classical' is used to describe the architecture of ancient Greece and Rome. For more than a hundred years educated men throughout the western world had been fascinated by these ancient buildings, notably the Parthenon and temples of Greece and the Colosseum of Rome. Their every detail was studied, their every measurement taken. So now, instead of asking a Scottish master mason to build a mansion, rich men would engage one of the new architects who had studied classical models in Italy. Their houses were all built by the same rules of the classical style. They were beautifully proportioned, with pillars and porticoes and large evenly spaced rectangular windows. At roof level they had triangles with sculptured groups, and sculptured friezes.

Too often these mansions did not fit so pleasingly into the Scottish background as the fortresses that had seemed to grow out of the solid rock. They were like hosts of others going up in all parts of the western world. They had their marble entrance halls, spacious drawing-rooms, dining-rooms and bedrooms, and their *salons*, elaborately carved and painted staircases, moulded ceilings and sculptured fireplaces— everything that could be desired in a classical mansion; but they were not Scottish. At Inveraray in the heart of the Highlands, the Duke of Argyll built a new castle about a hundred yards from the old stronghold. Born in England, educated at Eton, and a great statesman at Westminster, the Duke had little taste for things Scottish. His architect, an

Inveraray Castle

Englishman, designed a castle with what he thought were Scottish characteristics, and the result is a monstrosity in a 'mock-baronial' style.

The changes at Blair Castle were more pleasing. The old stronghold that had withstood many a siege, even as late as the 1745 Rebellion, was retained, but its rooms were modernised. A large wing was added on each side, in the classical style, blending with the central keep. The mansion's name was then changed to Blair House.

Johnson and Boswell visited Dunvegan Castle, in Skye, the home of the chief of the Macleods. They thought it a savage-looking place, with its vaulted cellars, great hall, and its cheerless bedrooms at the end of a weary climb to the top storey. But even this castle was being modernised. In 1790 alone, £4,000 was spent on repairing the old tower, building a new wing, putting in new windows, ornamental ceilings,

Dunvegan Castle

rainwater pipes and a new fireplace.

Nearer home, about three miles from Mauchline, 'where Lugar flows', Burns would see the masons building the stately home designed by Robert Adam for Lord Auchinleck, the father of Johnson's friend Boswell. Though not particularly large, it is beautifully proportioned, with its pillars, cornices and friezes, and handsome flight of steps to the front entrance —a delightful example of the classical style in miniature.

Auchinleck House

Every laird felt that he had to keep up with the times. The more prosperous built mansions on a smaller scale than the nobles. The poorer ones, the 'bonnet lairds', put up stone farmhouses, plain but substantial and comfortable. Wooden or stone floors, slated roofs, plastered walls and ceilings, built-in fireplaces, and larger glazed windows, were proof of progress. When Burns took over Ellisland Mr Miller advanced him money to build a new farmhouse, and the result was a great improvement on the 'auld clay biggin' ' in which he was born.

A surprising number of the architects were Scotsmen, some of them very famous. Sir William Bruce, who designed the middle section of Hopetoun House, and redesigned Holyrood Palace, had been King's Surveyor and Master of Works for Charles II. James Craig's layout of the new town of Edinburgh is still one of the finest examples of town

Hopetoun House

planning. Best known are William Adam and his three sons.
The father had worked in his early years with Sir William
Bruce, and the wings of Hopetoun House are his additions.
His eldest son, Robert, was the greatest of all the architects
of the age. He was so full of the traditions of Ancient Greece
and Rome that his creations were not just copies but great
original works in the classical style. Most of them were in
England, but he built over eighty mansions in the Scottish
countryside, besides many more in Edinburgh and Glasgow.
Culzean Castle in Ayrshire and Charlotte Square in Edinburgh are his Scottish masterpieces. Nowadays it is the
interiors that he designed that people admire most. They have
dignity, yet simplicity. The great staircases, rooms with
beautifully moulded *cornices* and ceilings, painted panels, and
perfectly proportioned windows and fireplaces, are lovely
to see.

Culzean Castle

Culzean Castle, the great staircase

78

A room in Culzean Castle

Furniture and Furnishings

Grand houses needed grand furniture and furnishings. The crude benches, stools and chairs, deal tables and chests which belonged to the old castles were completely out of place. Windows had to have expensive curtains, beds the finest linen and blankets and elaborately embroidered coverings. Wooden platters and pewter mugs might be good enough for the servants, but not for the laird and his family and guests.

The furniture was often designed by the architects to suit the new buildings. Some of the loveliest pieces were the work of Robert Adam. More often it was made by high class London cabinetmakers like Sheraton, Chippendale and Hepplewhite, from polished, gilded or lacquered mahogany.

Other pieces were imported from France, the work of craftsmen who made the furniture for the Court.

Floors were covered with expensive Wilton carpets. Though tapestries were still being woven, people now liked landscapes painted directly on to plastered walls or wooden panels. Much of the credit for this is due to a Scot, James Thomson. His poem 'Seasons' praising the countryside, was a great success when printed in London. It stimulated artists to make paintings of nature.

Imposing, in massive gilt frames, are priceless portraits by the most famous artists—the Scotsmen, Ramsay and Raeburn; the Englishmen, Gainsborough, Reynolds and Romney; the German-born Zoffany; and many other French, Italian and Dutch artists. A few yards from where Burns stayed in Edinburgh was the studio of Nasmyth, a struggling young artist. The poet and the painter became very friendly, and Burns was quite in the fashion when he had his portrait painted. This is the one reproduced on page 1. It is probably the truest likeness of him that we have.

When important guests were present meals were served on *delft* ware from Holland, or the new willow-pattern service from Stoke. The visitor no longer brought his own knife, fork and horn spoon; heavy solid silver cutlery was waiting him on the table. On the sideboard sat the elaborate four-gallon punch bowl from a new pottery at Glasgow, Portobello or Prestonpans. For the ladies' afternoon tea nothing less was good enough than the fabulously expensive egg-shell porcelain that had been brought all the way from China. Her Ladyship would do the washing up herself, for no servant could be trusted to handle these fragile tea dishes.

The music that followed was no longer accompanied by the pinging sound of the spinet or harpsichord. The ladies blended their voices with the notes of the newly invented pianoforte from London.

Clothing

Clothes must now be appropriate for elegant drawing-rooms. The 'hempen homespuns' would no longer do.

Gentlemen swaggered around with swords or gold-nobbed canes. Their coats, of finest English cloth, were tight at the waist, with long buttoned skirt, and cuffs reaching almost to the elbows. They were gaily embroidered with gold lace or with masses of flowers in natural colours. The ruffled shirt

Types of clothing worn by Scottish gentlemen

was of finest linen, the cravat of expensive lace. The short waistcoat was adorned with enormous gold, silver, glass or brass buttons as the occasion demanded. A gold *fob* dangled from the waist of the breeches. The legs were encased in red or yellow stockings. Many years had passed since a laird might be seen pacing across his land in his bare feet. His square-toed shoes, of finest tanned leather, were almost covered by outsize silver buckles.

Following the fashion of English gentlemen, heads and faces were clean-shaven, in day the baldness being covered by a wig, and at bedtime by a loose-fitting cap. A spare wig was kept in reserve, and these two cost as much as a farm-worker's wages for a year. The barber was a constant visitor to shave the male members of the family and dress their wigs. They massaged the curls with scented oil, then sprinkled them with powder. As the century came to an end men allowed their hair to grow long, slept with it in paper curlers, and when they sauntered forth it was tied at the back with a broad satin ribbon.

Nor were the ladies to be outdone by their friends in London. They still wore plaids, but, lined with silk, and draped gracefully over the shoulders, they were more for adornment than warmth. There was one difference: they wore no make-up, and visitors to Scotland commented with approval on the natural loveliness of their complexions. Except for this they got their fashions from the south. We read of them, or see their portraits, 'gorgeous in velvet or rustling in silk, and done up in all the accompaniments of fan, ear-rings, finger-rings, falling sleeves, scent bottles, embroidered bag, hoop and train'. Shot silk, trimmed with gauze or lace, was very popular. The hoops referred to, at the hem of the skirt, were enormous things, anything up to eight or nine feet in circumference, and requiring excellent

Types of clothing worn by Scottish ladies

steersmanship by the lady as she tilted it this way and that going through doorways or up and down narrow staircases. There is a story of a Jacobite seeking refuge under his true love's skirt until the Redcoats gave up the search. The shoes, with three inch high heels, were enlivened with gay little bows and ribbons. Nearer the end of the century hoops were smaller, or disappeared altogether, and skirts were draped on panniers on the hips.

The crowning glory was milady's hair. A silk-covered wire frame or a cushion a foot or more high was fixed on top of the head, and the hair was drawn up over it. The whole was then greased, powdered, and adorned with ribbons, rosettes or feathers to give it the final touch of distinctiveness.

Children's clothes were of the same coarse endurable material as before, except in company. Then the little fellows and their sisters were decked like adults in miniature.

Food and Drink
Food—and drink—now played a very important part in the life of the gentry. By the end of the century incredibly lavish meals had become the custom. It was an insult to one's host not to eat of every dish. Here is a typical breakfast table in a Scottish nobleman's home: oat cakes; barley bannocks; butter; cheeses; honey; red and black currant jelly; marmalade; preserved fruit; cream; eggs; fresh and salt herrings; boiled haddock and whiting; venison, beef, mutton and grouse; whisky, rum, brandy, claret, port, coffee and tea. The meal lasted two hours. For dinner there might be as many as sixty separate dishes, not including the appetiser immediately before it of bread, butter and cheese with smoked salmon or anchovies and a glass of brandy. Less wealthy people, of course, had fewer dishes, but even the bonnet lairds had their wheaten bread, their whisky, and a variety of cheeses, meats and fish.

With such prodigious eating went no less prodigious drinking. A visitor did not prove himself a true friend and a gentleman unless he sank dead drunk below the table. The servants then loosened his cravat to make sure he did not choke, and carried him off to bed. If there were a shortage of beds, a drawer in the chest would do as well. The servants in Castle Grant were gravely affronted on one occasion when a guest tottered upstairs by himself. One was heard muttering, 'Agh, it's sare changed times when a shentlemans can gang to bed on their ain feet.'

Education
With the ever-widening gulf between the rich and poor it was no longer good enough that the laird's son and the ploughman's son should sit at the same desk in the parish school. There was no fit education there for a gentleman. Besides, many of the lairds no longer lived on their estates; they spent their time in Edinburgh, London or abroad. Two thirds of Scotland was owned by such absentee landlords. Merchants who had made fortunes in the Glasgow tobacco trade or cotton trade, or as servants of the East India Company, bought estates of bankrupt spendthrift lairds. The close-knit community that had been so common in Scotland was splitting apart, and young men and girls from the landowning class had to be educated for a higher society.

In the bigger houses there might be a tutor at home, a young clergyman who had not yet been called to a church of his own. He was treated contemptuously as a servant, and often paid less than one. When the boy was old enough to go to college or grammar school the tutor would accompany him—to Edinburgh, Perth or Glasgow—and stay with him to supervise his studies. By the end of the century it was becoming more common for the laird to buy or rent a house near the school, and the whole family would migrate there for the term.

After a few years the young man proceeded to one of the Scottish universities, or, if the family were wealthy enough, to Oxford or Cambridge, or even to one of the well-known European universities. Holidays provided an opportunity to travel abroad, to 'learn *bon ton* and see the world', as Burns so aptly put it. The Scottish youths tended to take their education more seriously than their English counterparts, and Dr Johnson was amazed to find so many, even in remote Highland areas, who were so widely read, and could discuss philosophy and religion and quote the classic authors.

Here is an actual educational scheme worked out by a Mr Dempster for his seven-year-old nephew. The tutor would go to college with him, then to university, and would accompany him on his travels. Until he was twelve he would attend grammar school, spending his holidays on the estate, riding, shooting, fishing, visiting the neighbouring gentry, and getting to know the tenants. For the next three years he would be at St Andrews University, visiting Edinburgh, Glasgow, England and North Wales during the vacations. When sixteen he would go to Edinburgh University to study law—so necessary for estate management—and spend his holidays in London and the south of England, in Ireland and in Europe. By the time he was seventeen or eighteen he would have his degree. Yes, much more was crammed into the young years than we should approve of today.

As for the laird's daughter, she had a governness to teach her to read, write, sew, and keep the household accounts. She would then go to a 'finishing school' to learn embroidery, ballroom dancing, music, and the care of a house and servants. Some weeks might be spent at a 'pastry school' discovering the finer points of baking, cake decoration, and sweet-making. All this, of course, was by way of preparation for an eligible marriage and a home of her own.

6 The Growth of Trade and Industry

Until the eighteenth century not only was Scotland's farming very backward, but she had very little trade and industry. The total tonnage leaving Scottish ports with their cargoes of salt herring, salmon, pladding, stockings, candles and rope was about 6,000. The biggest ship was 180 tons.

This is a model of a ship that sailed from Glasgow to Virginia and the West Indies

The Scottish parliament agreed to join the English parliament in 1707 mainly because Scotland was promised free trade with England and England's colonies. Glasgow developed a very profitable trade in tobacco from Virginia, and sugar from the West Indies. But this was not enough. Industries had to be set up to provide goods for export.

The government encouraged the linen trade. They paid farmers to grow flax, and we have seen that the Burns family did quite well at Lochlea as a result. In every part of the country linen yarn was being spun and cloth being woven in the cottages of the peasants, and later in factories in the towns. By 1800 the manufacture of linen was over twenty-one million yards a year compared with not much more than one million in 1700.

The woollen industry was also flourishing. From Ayrshire, Glasgow, Aberdeen and Fife came plaids, bonnets, carpets, stockings and blankets for export to England, Europe and America.

The American War of Independence (1776 to 1783) dealt a severe blow to the tobacco trade, but a new industry grew up to bring prosperity to the nation. This was the manufacture of cotton yarn and cloth. Newly invented spinning machines driven by water power led to factories being built wherever there was a swift stream to turn the mill-wheels.

The mill wheel in Arkwright's factory

Flax was too sticky to be used on these machines. Besides, cotton cloth was cheaper than linen, because it did not need such a long and costly bleaching process. It was light, gay and easily washed. Glasgow and Páisley became the centres of cotton manufacture, Glasgow alone had 2,000 looms by 1800, and exported four or five million yards of cotton cloth.

In 1759, the year in which Burns was born, the first important ironworks was built in Scotland, at Carron, near Falkirk. Two great discoveries had made this possible. The

A hand loom

first was that if coal were heated until all the impurities were driven off—that is, if it were coked—it could be used for *smelting* iron. Before that, charred wood—charcoal—was used; but wood had become very scarce. The second was that there was very good ironstone in the Forth-Clyde valley, beside an abundant supply of coal. Within a few years the Carron Ironworks was turning out ploughs, spades, grates, stoves, pots, railings, cannons and cannonballs. The greatest

A carronade at the Tower of London

James Watt, whose improved steam engine prepared the way for the Industrial Revolution

single invention was the new type of steam engine invented by James Watt in 1765 to pump water out of the coal mines. He soon adapted it to the driving of machinery, and this led to a great increase in factory production. It is not surprising that historians call these changes an 'Industrial Revolution'.

Until the middle of the century the Clyde was a sluggish river spreading over the flat land and round many little islands and sandbanks. At Glasgow Bridge at low tide it was only fifteen inches deep. No ship of more than five tons could come within fourteen miles of the city. A two-way traffic of rafts and flat-bottomed barges, or ponies trekking along the narrow paths alongside the river, carried the goods to and from Port Glasgow, over twenty miles away. The increase in trade made it absolutely necessary to deepen the river. This was done by building jetties to narrow it, and the force of the tide swept the sand downstream, to be removed by dredging. On his rare visits to Glasgow, Burns, standing on the new Jamaica Bridge, could see ships sailing right up to the Broomielaw.

In 1790 the Forth and Clyde Canal, and its branch the Monkland Canal, were opened. Goods from the whole valley could be exported from the east or west to every part of the world.

New hard-surfaced roads, built and kept in repair by charges paid at the toll-houses, or 'turnpikes', allowed heavy loads to be carried by carts in every direction. Passenger traffic became speedier. In 1700 the journey from Glasgow to Edinburgh took two days; in 1800 it could be done in six hours. Between 1750 and 1800 over 3,000 miles of turnpike roads were built in Scotland.

So many people had flocked to the towns of the south to look for jobs—Highlanders, small farmers, and even Irishmen —that employers, always sure of plenty of workers, paid very low wages. Women and children could easily be trained to do factory work, and it was quite usual to employ great numbers of them. The working day, for men, women and children, was very long: more than fourteen hours, for six days on end, with 8s. for men, 4s. for women, and 2s. for children at the end of the week. The factory conditions, too, would appear shocking to us. The workers had to keep on their feet all the time, even when eating their scrappy meals, and were not allowed to talk to one another. The air was damp and hot, for this was the atmosphere needed to keep the cotton threads from breaking.

Even worse were the conditions in the coal mines. Miners and their families belonged to the mine-owner. They were not free to go to other areas or to other jobs. It was not until 1799 that they were freed. The father and his elder sons set out in the early hours to hew the coal. His wife, daughters

and younger sons followed soon after, to heap the coal into trucks that were drawn to the foot of the shaft by ponies, or, more often, by the children crawling on all fours. In some mines the women and older girls carried the coal, more than a hundredweight and a half at a time, in baskets on their backs, the mother leading the way with a lighted candle in her teeth. We read of them staggering 150 yards to the foot of the pit, climbing up stairs for more than 100 feet, then on to the dump, and doing this no fewer than twenty-four times in a day's work.

Women Coal bearers

No doubt the growth of industry and trade brought great wealth to factory owners, mine-owners and merchants; but for a long time it caused fearful hardship to the working people. It is not surprising that in the last years of the eighteenth century they were in a rebellious mood.

7 Burns the Rebel

Scotland in the lifetime of Burns was becoming a country in which wealthy people could live elegantly, and rich landlords could make money from the land. But it was also a land of desperately poor farmers, of homeless people turned

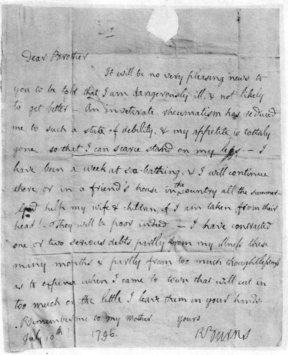

Burns's last letter to his brother Gilbert

off the land and swarming beggars. Burns felt that he belonged with the unfortunate. Although he visited the grand folk at Castle Gordon and Atholl House, he ended up in a little house in Dumfries, struggling against poverty and rheumatic

> Robt Burns was born at Alloway in
> the parish of Ayr — Jan.ʸ 25ᵗʰ 1759 —
> Jean Armour his wife was born at Mauchline
> Feb.ʸ 27.ᵗʰ 1767 —
>
> Sepl. 3: 1786 were born to them twins, Robert, their
> eldest Son, at a quarter past Noon & Jean since
> dead at fourteen months old. — March 3, 1788 were born
> to them twins again, two daughters who died within a
> few days after their birth. — August 18ᵗʰ 1789 was
> born to them, Francis Wallace; so named after
> Mrs Dunlop of Dunlop; he was born a quarter
> before seven, forenoon. — April 9ᵗʰ 1791 between
> three & four in the morning, was born to them
> William Nicol; so named after Mr Wm Nicol of the
> High School Edin. — November 21ˢᵗ 1792 at
> a quarter past Noon, was born to them Elizabeth Riddel,
> so named after Mrs Robt Riddel of Glenriddel. —

Entries by Burns in the family Bible

fever. When he died in 1796 he was wretchedly poor and in debt, shunned and neglected. Why did he die so unhappily after becoming so famous?

Most writers think that Burns brought his troubles on his own head. They say that he had been too bold in his criticism of the Church and its Holy Willies, that he was too fond of the girls, even after he was married, that he had become a drunkard, and, most important of all, he had insulted too many important people.

There is some truth in all these charges. Objecting to its interference in the lives of the people, he had made the

93

The house in Dumfries where Burns died

Church a laughing stock, and held up to ridicule its hypo-
crites and humbugs. The ministers got their own back by
spreading exaggerated stories of his drunkenness and evil
living in the hope that the people would not be influenced
by what he had written. He did have too many girl friends,
probably because they were attracted by his charms. At times
he did drink more than his weak stomach could stand. But
when we compare the conduct of Burns with that of many
in his own day we see that he was no worse than others.
Judges, Cabinet Ministers, so-called gentlemen, and even
clergymen, felt no shame at appearing drunk in public, and
they, too, were excessively fond of female company. Burns
knew his own weaknesses, and this gave him added sympathy
for those who fell by the wayside:

'Then gently scan your brother man,
    Still gentler sister woman;
Though they may gang a kenning wrang,
    To step aside is human.'

It is true that he had denounced and insulted many important people—the king, his ministers, and members of his court, for example—but only because he honestly believed that the people were suffering from their government. 'Sic a parcel of rogues in a nation', he sneered. He had known what the penalty would be, for even at the height of his fame he had written in a letter:

'I am determined to flatter no created being. I set as little by kings, lords, clergy, critics, etc., as all those respectable gentry do by *bardship*. I know what I may expect from the world, by and by; illiberal abuse, and perhaps contemptuous neglect.'

'*Affliction's Sons are Brothers in Distress*' ('A Winter's Night') The honesty of Burns's criticism, his hatred of oppression, snobbery, bigotry, hypocrisy and poverty, is the main reason for his troubles. He was a man of the people. He knew them, he understood them, he loved them, and was heartsore and angry when he saw their poverty and misery. The poor were in a mood for rebellion, and were demanding a share in government, in the hope that in this way they could improve their lot.

Life had always been hard for the working people in Scotland, but, as we have seen, the changes in farming and industry were making it harder still. As a result of the Enclosures thousands had been driven from their farms, and forced to take work as farm labourers, or to look for jobs in the new factories. There was just not enough work for all who were looking for it so desperately, especially as so many women and children were employed in the factories. The lucky ones who did get jobs had to be content with just enough wages to keep them alive. Many, especially older men, would never have work again. There were still thousands begging from house to house, and the roads were infested with *vagrants*, many of whom had to resort to thieving and violence.

It was no use appealing to the government to improve conditions, for it was the great landowners, merchants and factory-owners who were the members of parliament. The ordinary people had no say in their election; there were only 2,624 voters in the whole of Scotland. In the towns, only members of the Council had the vote; in the country only the great landowners. So absurd was the situation that in Bute the Sheriff was the only voter, and he elected himself to parliament. Edinburgh was the only Scottish town with a member of its own. In other cases one M.P. represented several towns. Glasgow, Renfrew, Rutherglen and Dumbarton shared the same member, and he was elected by a group of four men, one from each of the Councils.

To the Scots England was still 'the auld enemy'. They felt that the parliament in London was determined to keep them poor. They had no faith in the Scottish members, for they always voted as the Prime Minister told them to—and were well bribed to do so. They had no sympathy for the poor in Scotland.

Never had a king and his government been so unpopular, even in England, as at the end of the eighteenth century. From time to time George III became mad and had to be locked up. The men chosen to govern Scotland in his name, like Henry Dundas, the Home Secretary, and Lord Braxfield, the Chief Justice, were ruthless and merciless.

It was the tyranny of the king that finally drove the Americans to rebellion. The sympathy of the Scots was with the Americans, and the unemployment and starvation that resulted from the war was blamed on the king and his government. Burns risked imprisonment, transportation to Botany Bay in Australia, or even execution, by writing, in 'an Ode for General Washington's Birthday':

'See gathering thousands, while I sing,
  A broken chain exulting bring,
    And dash it in a tyrant's face.'
The 'tyrant', of course, was George the Third.

In 1789 the French people, who had been suffering even greater poverty and tyranny, turned against their royal family and the aristocrats, and set up their own government. For hundreds of years—until it was ended by the Act of Union in 1707—the Scots had an 'Auld Alliance' with the French. They rejoiced that their old allies had gained their freedom, and formed secret societies to help them, and if possible to win the same freedom for the Scots. Burns showed his sympathy more openly. He bought three *carronades* from a smuggling ship that he had helped to capture, and sent them to the revolutionary government in France. They were seized before they could leave Scotland, and Burns was summoned before the Excise Commissioners on a charge of 'having a leaning to democracy', a grave crime that could be punished by death. His defence, 'I feel that corruptions have set in, which every patriotic Briton desires to be amended', caused great offence. Only an appeal for mercy by one or two powerful friends who had not yet deserted him saved him from a severe sentence. He was warned to act, not to think, and to be silent and obedient. There was no possibility now of the promotion in his job that he had been promised earlier.

Year by year sympathy for the French became more dangerous. The government knew how they were hated, and were afraid that success of the French Revolution would lead to a similar uprising in Britain. Their fears were increased when the French guillotined their king and queen and their children. Louis XVI and his queen Marie Antoinette had been found guilty of treason for inviting Austrian armies to help them against their own people. The execution of hosts

97

of French aristocrats followed. The last straw, as far as the British Government was concerned, was when the French called on the people of the world to rise against tyranny, and promised military aid to those who did so. A rebellion in Ireland followed immediately, and it was feared that the Scots, too, would rise. Britain declared war against France.

The government took powers to arrest and sentence without trial any person suspected of wanting to change the form of government, or of sympathy for the French. Even

Lord Braxfield, Chief Justice

when a trial was held, the verdict of 'Guilty' was a foregone conclusion. The chief judge, Lord Justice Clerk Braxfield, is reported to have said to a juror before a trial, 'Come awa', and help to hang ane o' thae damned scoondrels.' Spies were everywhere, reporting even private conversations. The Scots were dealt with particularly severely. Sentences to death by hanging, to slavery in Botany Bay, and to long terms of imprisonment, became increasingly common.

After the warnings he had been given, Burns had to be more careful of what he did and said in public. He was not afraid for himself, but he could not risk sacrificing his family. Yet nothing could prevent him from putting his indignation into his poetry. Typical of his opinions are the lines he had

scratched earlier on a window pane in Stirling Castle:
'The injured Stewart race is gone,
A race outlandish fills their throne:
An idiot race, to honour lost—
Who know them best despise them most.'
Now, in 1793, he went even further, in 'Scots wha hae'. On the surface this appears to be Bruce's appeal to his soldiers to fight bravely against the English at Bannockburn. But, as Burns wrote to a friend, 'it was inspired by struggles of the same nature, not quite so ancient'. The proud usurper he had in mind was not Edward I but George III. Better 'a gory bed' than 'chains and slavery' was a call to revolution.

In 'A Man's a Man for a' that', written just a year before he died, he poured out his contempt for the ruling class. He believed it was the quality of people alone that mattered. In time all men would be equal, and there would be peace and justice throughout the world:
'What though on hamely fare we dine—
Wear hodden grey, and a' that?
Gie fools their silks, and knaves their wine—
A man's a man for a' that:
For a' that and a' that,
Their tinsel show, and a' that;
The honest man, though e'er sae poor,
Is king o' men for a' that.

. . .

Then let us pray that come it may,
As come it will for a' that,
That sense and worth, o'er a' the earth,
May bear the gree and a' that:
For a' that, and a' that,
It's comin' yet for a' that,
That man to man, the warld o'er,
Shall brothers be for a' that.

Burns's wife, Jean Armour, in her later years

It is not surprising that his noble friends of the Edinburgh days wanted nothing more to do with him, and that those who still loved and admired him were afraid to be seen in his company. He felt his loneliness keenly. We can hear his anguish in one of his loveliest songs, written shortly before his death:

> Ye banks and braes o' bonie Doon,
>> How can ye bloom sae fresh and fair!
> How can ye chant, ye little birds,
>> And I sae weary, fu' o' care!'

Now we can understand why Burns is so beloved in Scotland, and indeed by peoples throughout the world. He was of the people. He knew their every mood. He laughed with them. He laughed at them. He sorrowed with them. He spoke for them; and by appealing to them through his poems and songs he did more than any other man to bring about—long after his death—the democracy of which we are so proud today.

Many thousands, from all over the country, followed him through the streets of Dumfries to his last resting-place, expressing to him in death what they had been afraid to express in the last years of his life.

Burns's funeral

Ashamed of their treatment of Burns, the people of Dumfries made amends by turning his home into a museum, and by building a handsome tomb over his grave. The 'Mausoleum', as the tomb is called, is like a very small Greek temple. Inside it, on the back wall, is a sculptured marble panel showing the young ploughman being inspired by the muse of poetry. Every year thousands visit the house and the mausoleum to pay homage to Scotland's bard.

PROSE VERSIONS OF THE POEMS QUOTED

The following passages are simple prose versions of the poetry quoted in this book. The page on which the poetry appears is shown in brackets.

(6) She is always clean and neat in her dress, respectable and graceful; but then, there is something in her bearing that makes any dress that she wears look well.   ('Handsome Nell')

(8) It is hardly in a person's power to keep at times from being sour to see how things are shared.   ('Epistle to Davie')

(9) Our landlord gets in his extortionate rents, his coals, his share of the tenants' produce and everything that is due him. He gets out of his bed at any time he wants. His servants come when he rings for them. He has just to call for his coach or his horse. He pulls out a long silken purse full of golden guineas peeping through the meshes.   ('The Twa Dogs')

(9) A cottager digging in a ditch, building a wall with dirty stones, digging in a quarry, and doing other hard jobs like that, barely manages to provide for himself and his wife and a swarm of half-naked children. It is only by such hand-labour that he can provide the thatch and rope to keep a roof over their heads.   ('The Twa Dogs')

(21) She was no child of moorland rams, with matted fleece and hairy hips, for her ancestors were brought in ships from south of the River Tweed.   ('Poor Mailie's Elegy')

(29) I greatly pity anyone who is staying here unless he has come as a servant to the great and mighty duke.
There is nothing here but Highland pride and Highland skin-disease and starvation. If fate sent me here, it was surely because it was angry with me.   ('Lines written at Inveraray')

(46) There, lonely, huddled by the fireside, I sat and gazed at the foul smoke belching forth and filling the old clay house with acrid fumes that made me cough, and listening to the rats scurrying about the rafters.   ('The Vision')

(49) In the long run, the worst that can happen is to become a beggar.   ('Epistle to Davie')

102

(56) As they make love, exchange witty sallies, and enjoy the fun of company, they forget that there is anxiety in the world. ('The Twa Dogs')

(57) The ale is covered with bubbling froth, and a steam rises from it to warm the heart. The well-drawing pipe and the snuff-box are handed round with right good will. ('The Twa Dogs')

(65) His coat is the same colour as his handsome bonnet, his shirt as white as new-driven snow, his stockings are blue, his shoes as black as sloeberries, and his clear silver buckles dazzle us all. ('The Ronalds of the Bennals')

(68) As the chill winds of November blow loudly with an angry whistle, and the shortening winter's day is coming to an end, the oxen, mud-caked, come from the plough, and clouds of crows, blackening the sky, fly back to their nests. The cottager, tired out by his labour, goes home; tonight a week's drudgery is at an end. He collects his tools—spade, mattock and hoes— hoping to spend the next day resting, at ease. Weary, he makes his way homeward across the moor.
   After a time he comes in sight of his lonely cottage sheltered beneath an aged tree. The little toddlers, waiting for their father, stagger along to meet him with fluttering cries of delight. The pleasant surroundings, with the blinking fire, the clean hearth, the smile of his thrifty wife, and the baby sitting prattling on his knee, make him quite forget his cares and anxiety and his toil. ('The Cotter's Saturday Night')

(68) The youngsters are told to obey the commands of their masters and mistresses, to do their work with a diligent hand, and never, even when out of sight, to dodge or play. And be sure always to obey the Lord. ('The Cotter's Saturday Night')

(70) I could see in him no more pride, vanity or dignity than in an honest ploughman. ('To Lord Daer')

(71) From morning till evening it is nothing but baking, roasting, frying, boiling. ('The Twa Dogs')

(94) Then gently examine your brother man, and still more gently sister woman. Though they may go off the straight and narrow path a little, that's a human failing, after all.
                                   ('Address to the Unco Guid')

(99) Does it really matter if we eat simple food, wear clothes made of home-made cloth, and so on? Let fools have their silks and knaves their wines. It is really the character of a man that matters. Despite all their gaudy trash, the honest man, no matter how poor, is king of men, for all that . . .

Then let us pray that it will come about—as it must, in spite of all difficulties—that sense and worth will be looked on as the most important qualities. The time must come when men in every part of the world will be brothers.

('A Man's a Man for a' that')

(100) You banks and slopes of lovely Doon, how can you bloom so fresh and fair! How can you chant, you little birds, when I am so weary and full of care! ('Ye Banks and Braes')

The interior of Burns's mausoleum, Dumfries

THINGS TO DO

1. Find a book of Burns's poems and read some more for yourself. Make your own glossary of the special words he uses and find out their meanings.

2. Read two more books in the 'Then and There' series: 'Tobacco Lords of Glasgow' and 'The Golden Age of Edinburgh'. Discuss in class whether town or country life has changed more in Scotland since the eighteenth century.

3. In 'The Twa Dogs' Burns makes his two dogs discuss the contrasts in the way people live. Write your own conversation between two dogs (in prose or verse) either about the differences between Highland and Lowland living or between the rich and the poor.

4. Imagine you are taking a trip on horseback first through the Lowlands and then the Highlands in the days of Burns. Write a diary of all the things you notice on the way.

5. Find out more about (a) the American Revolution (b) the French Revolution (you can read two 'Then and There' books on these subjects). Then have a class discussion on why Burns was on the side of the Americans and the French in their rebellion against their governments.

GLOSSARY

balk, grass strip separating one man's land from another's in the infield
baneful, harmful
bardship, being a bard or poet
bawbee, halfpenny
bon ton, French for good manners
buss, fishing ship of about ninety tons
cantraip, a witch's spell
carronade, short cannon made in the Carron Ironworks
cascrom, wooden spade tipped with iron
chaise, light, open carriage
claymore, large sword
cornice, plaster moulding between ceiling and wall
cottar, *cotter*, farm-worker

crofter, small farmer owning a croft
cupples, stout branches forming the roof framing
delft, pottery made at Delft in Holland
dirk, dagger
distaff, stick on which was placed wool or flax for spinning
divot, tuft of grass
dominie, schoolmaster
dormer, small window in the roof
duffel or *duffle*, thick, coarse, woollen cloth
to extirpate, to kill off completely or destroy
fob, chain with seals, etc. hanging on it
foray, quick expedition to steal cattle, etc.
henchman, servant or follower
Jacobite, follower of James Stuart
infield, land nearest to the farm on which the main crops were grown
kelp, seaweed or the ashes of burnt seaweed
kelpie, evil water-spirit
Kirk Session, meeting of leaders of the Church (Kirk)
mensal, Highland chieftain's estate
mutch, woman's cap
outfield, land lying away from the farm house, mainly pasture
pladding, flannel
presbytery, meeting of ministers and elders of the Church
putrid, bad, rotten
reiver, robber
rotation, a regular order in which things change, here change of crops
salon, large drawing-room
say, coarse home-woven cloth
scunnered, disgusted
sedan chair, covered chair, carried by two chairmen
smelt, to, to melt metal in order to separate it from stone, etc.
sorner, thief who gets money, etc., by threats
spunkie, spirit
tack, land held by lease
targe, shield
trumpery, something which deceives
vagrant, tramp, one with no settled dwelling
vendetta, revenge or a blood feud
warlock, wizard
winding sheet, cloth in which a dead body was wrapped for burial
wraith, ghost